N. F. S.
GRUNDTVIG

Selected Writings

N.F.S. GRUNDTVIG

Edited and with an Introduction by
Johannes Knudsen

Translated by
Johannes Knudsen
Enok Mortensen
Ernest D. Nielsen

FORTRESS PRESS   Philadelphia

Library of Congress Catalog Card Number 76–007873
ISBN 0–8006–1238–8

5721D76   Printed in U.S.A.   1-1238

Contents

Preface

The translation of N. F. S. Grundtvig has come late. In contrast to his Danish contemporary Søren Kierkegaard, whose writings lured translators by their elegant style, Grundtvig is difficult to translate. His prose is long-drawn, repetitious, and cumbersome. His poetry is so filled with concentrated and poetic imagery and is so pregnant with meaning that it places great demands upon the translator for understanding and poetic ability.

The reason for this modest effort to introduce Grundtvig's thought to the public in the English language is that there has been a continuous and growing demand for such an undertaking. As Kierkegaard met the needs for individual self-examination that characterized the pre–World War II period, Grundtvig now appeals to the corporate and historic emphases in the understanding of Christianity that prevail today. Moreover, Grundtvig's educational vision is sought as much as ever. Thirty years ago Bishop Anders Nygren of Sweden prophesied: Kierkegaard comes first; then Grundtvig.

HARRY C. JENSEN
JOHANNES KNUDSEN
ENOK MORTENSEN
ERNEST D. NIELSEN

Introduction
by JOHANNES KNUDSEN

The writings of N. F. S. Grundtvig must be read in the context of his life and time. This is, of course, true of all writers and prophets, but it is true of Grundtvig in a peculiar way. In contrast to Kierkegaard, whose writings, even the philosophical ones, reflect the immediate environment and experiences of the author, Grundtvig addresses himself to universal and broadly historical themes. These do not, as a whole, reflect personal concerns, although such concerns are not absent. It is the nature and history of the Christian life and the church, the nature and involvement of man, the implications of folk-life and culture, and the need for imaginative and expansive education that concerned him. Nevertheless, Grundtvig was so totally immersed in the engagements of his time and his people, and he developed his viewpoints so intimately in relation to these, that the background is always necessary for understanding. He was, furthermore, in so volatile a progressive development of new attitudes and points of view that his writings must be judged by the period and the situation in which they were authored. It is therefore necessary to give a brief sketch of his career in order to place his writings in context.

Nikolaj Frederik Severin Grundtvig, born in 1783, was the third son of a Lutheran pastor and his wife, and the descendant, through both parents, of a long line of ministers. Through his family, his education, and his involvement in the church as well as the culture of his country he was intensely Danish and Lutheran. He was also very much a child of his time, an age shaped by the philosophical heritage of the eighteenth century, the romantic and philosophical innovations of the nineteenth, the political currents of Europe from the French Revolution to the Franco-Prussian War, and the rising

1

political and social concerns of the post-Metternich period. The scope of this summary is underscored by the fact that he was born in 1783 and died in 1872 at almost eighty-nine years of age. It is interesting to note that Grundtvig was thirty years old when Kierkegaard was born, and that he outlived Kierkegaard by seventeen years.

After a dull academic career in which he studied theology rather haphazardly before receiving a degree, he came explosively alive in his early twenties when three factors jolted him: an unrequited and soul-shaking love affair, the tragic defeats of his country in the war with England in 1807, and the discovery of world literature and the new philosophies of his own century. For a while he immersed himself in poetic and historical effort with a strongly nationalistic interest in history and mythology. Later in his twenties he was drawn into a pastoral career, but suffered through an acutely emotional, even psychotic, crisis of a religious nature which could be called an intense conversion experience and which made him a fervent champion of traditional Lutheranism. His critical bent and his impulsive nature made his career in the church a turbulent one, and he spent years subsidized by scholarships and engaged in historical research and the translations of ancient Nordic documents. At the same time he was engaged in philosophical inquiry, probing the leading minds of the eighteenth and nineteenth centuries. The literary efforts of these years will not be included in this volume of translations.

In the middle of the 1820s, when he was in his early forties and when Kierkegaard was not yet confirmed, he experienced a breakthrough of religious assurance and understanding of considerable magnitude and far-reaching significance. His problem had been one of religious certainty and religious authority. Philosophically he had investigated and exhausted the ideas of the eighteenth century, being influenced mostly by John Locke. He had also absorbed the new ideas of the nineteenth century, particularly those of Friederich W. J. von Schelling. Theologically, Grundtvig had been traditionally Lutheran and biblical. His upsetting concern was the erosion of Christian certainties and traditional teachings by the so-called rationalists in the church. In his protest against their rejection of creedal teachings he, as others, had argued from biblical texts. To his dismay and concern, however, it became obvious that the "enemy" used the same Bible, claiming its authority for their arguments. At times his spirit was very low.

Then, in the mid-1820s, he was filled with a new experience of Christian hope which was reflected in poetry and hymn-writing, one example of which is the magnificent hymn, "O Day Full of Grace." Influenced by the writings of the church father Irenaeus, the insight came to him that his Christian faith was not based on an adequate compilation and interpretation of biblical texts but on the faith and proclamation of the church in its worship, especially in the sacraments. Acting upon this new insight and assurance, he impulsively launched an attack upon a theological professor, H. N. Clausen, a disciple of Schleiermacher, who had published a theological analysis of Catholicism and Protestantism. The attack was published under the title "The Response of the Church," and it is with excerpts from this document that we begin our prose translations. Grundtvig expressed himself strongly, so harshly, in fact, that he was placed under censorship by the courts, and although the basic idea prevailed his "matchless discovery," as he called it, must be studied in the light of later developments.

Under discipline by the church as well as by the civil government, Grundtvig again applied himself to historical and theological writings. He published lengthy essays on the nature of Christianity and the relation to the Lutheran tradition. These essays reflect two important emphases. The one emphasis was the call for what we today would call an "existential theology." In two of these essays, "The Truth of Christianity" and "True Christianity," Grundtvig posed the existential question almost two decades before Kierkegaard took it up. The second emphasis was Grundtvig's serious questioning whether traditional Lutheranism was adequate for the nineteenth century. He published an essay entitled "Shall the Lutheran Reformation Be Continued?" Even as he wrote these essays, however, his mind was in a turmoil of further development; he even ended one series of articles, later published as a single essay, by refuting what he had written in an earlier installment. The language of these essays is cumbersome and the conclusions are often clarified or even superseded by later insights; they have therefore been bypassed in this volume of translation.

In 1829–31 Grundtvig made three trips to England to study ancient Anglo-Saxon manuscripts. These trips had a strong effect upon him, for he experienced the British type of university education and he was removed from the parochial atmosphere of a small country whose economic life had been stagnant for two decades. There, too, he saw the hustle of the industrial revolution in its British beginnings. He began to think in terms of that active participation in public life which characterized the next two decades, even leading him into parliament after the granting of a new constitution in 1849. He began to see the need for a confrontation of social and cultural factors with basic Christianity, and out of this confrontation came the call for a "civic and noble academy." This again led to his fundamental educational writings, in which he proposed schools for the people and thus fostered the famous Danish folk schools. Selections from these writings are included in this volume.

For the moment, however, Grundtvig was occupied by a new engagement with Nordic mythology, a natural consequence of his British studies. In the introduction to a volume on the subject, he worked through the budding ideas of the relation of culture and Christianity. He revised this introduction many times, and all of the revisions are deposited in the Royal Danish Archives. They have been thoroughly researched by Kaj Thaning in his monumental, 776-page dissertation *Menneske Først ("Man First")*. In light of Thaning's analysis, Grundtvig's forementioned Introduction, published 1832, now looms as a significant milestone in his thought, and we have selected nineteen of its 170 pages for translation. Here we find, at times in rudimentary form, many of Grundtvig's later ideas. Most of all, this introduction marks a change of emphasis in his writing and thinking.

The analysis of this turnaround has led to various and disputed interpretations. Kaj Thaning, who has made the most thorough study, suggests in his recent book that Grundtvig moved from his emphasis on a personal religion in the historic fellowship of worship and launched into a strong emphasis on culture and temporal liv-

ing.[1] Others view Grundtvig's turnabout as a more consistent
evolution. A modern note has entered this discussion by the use of
terms related to the trend toward secularization, and this raises a
semantic problem for translators, exemplified by the English version
of Thaning's book. The Danish language allows for a distinction
between "secularization" and "secularizing," which cannot as readily
be made in English. In its application to Grundtvig the first term
would mean that the Christian approach to life is abandoned for an
exclusively human or humanistic approach. The second would
mean that Christian efforts are turned toward an effective realization
of the faith in the world of human problems. Interpreters with an
existential or even a Marxist approach prefer the former term, others
choose the second term, a position taken by the translators of this
volume. We would concur that when Grundtvig said "man first
and then Christian" he did not mean that human living has primacy
over Christian living but rather that the humanity of individual
living and of the indigenous life of a people, created in the image of
God, has a primary influence upon Christian experience and fellowship. Basically there can be no dichotomy of human living and
Christian living.

In this connection it must be noted that Grundtvig placed great
emphasis upon the cultural fellowship of a people united by history,
geography, and nationality. He calls this fellowship "folk-life," a
term which we discuss in more detail in connection with the translations. The term is inadequate in American parlance, where "folk"
usually is connected with a rural and unsophisticated culture. For
Grundtvig it meant, mainly in connection with the religious life,
that Christianity must be indigenous to the life of a people. Especially in its worship, Christianity is not a matter of individual
concern alone; it is a community life which finds its earthly home in
the human forms for common values that have grown in various

1. Kaj Thaning, N. F. S. Grundtvig (Copenhagen, 1972): "He had . . . received an answer
to his question as to the meaning of the course of a person's life and that of the life of the
human race. The answer was that it meant everything, both to God, who created life, and
therefore to man, who has to live it. Christianity exists for the salvation of human life, its
purpose being, not to liberate man from life, but for life. The Christian gospel could free man
from his bonds, his enemies, sin, which is self-will, and from darkness, which is the adversary
of life and death, which threatens and finally destroys all living things." (Kaj Thaning, N. F.
S. Grundtvig, trans. David Hohnen [Copenhagen, 1972], p. 83.)

parts of our created world. This corporate aspect, which was absent in Kierkegaard's agonizing search for Christian living and which he rejected in his philosophical as well as his devotional writings, is essential to Grundtvig's understanding of the Christian life.

In 1839, at the age of fifty-six, Grundtvig was appointed pastor of the chapel in the Vartov home for the aged. It was the worship in the sanctuary of this institution, located in the inner city two blocks from Kierkegaard's childhood home, that became the congregational home for a great number of people influenced by his ideas and especially by his hymn-writing. He preached at Vartov for the next thirty-three years. The printed sermons from this period offer significant insights into his thought, and we are including a selected number of them in this volume. It is important to note what a man says in his proclamation of the gospel, especially a man whose public writings often are quite polemical.

Grundtvig continued to write and participate in public life until the day before his death in September 1872. During the strong attack by Kierkegaard upon the Danish church in 1954-55 he remained silent, perhaps out of deference to the agony of Kierkegaard's crisis. Later on he took up the attack for consideration in his sermons as well as in theological treatises. We have tried to select sermons that illustrate this. From his seventy-second to his seventy-eighth year he wrote a series of essays in which he summarized his views of Christianity and the church. He called these *The Christian Childhood Teachings;* we have titled the published collection "Basic Christian Teachings." These essays are plainly written by an old man who is looking to the past. They are verbose and repetitious, even garrulous, and they have a tendency toward dogmatization. In fact, they offer an interesting insight into the mind of a great man who lives long enough to dogmatize himself. On the other hand, they reveal a mature insight and reflection often missing in earlier and more polemical documents, together with the wisdom and profundity of age. We are publishing a number of essays from this series.

In these later essays Grundtvig expresses his basic views of the church and its gospel, stressing that the salvatory word of the gospel is a "word from the mouth of the Lord" at baptism and Communion.

He ties this to the confession of faith, and although he denies in a late document that this Word is to be identified with *Symbolum Apostolicum* or the Apostles' Creed, this has been a common and traditional interpretation of his position. The expression "from the mouth of the Lord" has led to theories that Jesus dictated the creed to the apostles during the forty days between the resurrection and the ascension. Such a theory was proposed by Rufinus in the fourth century and by Lessing in the eighteenth. The idea appealed to Grundtvig, at least for a time, and some of his followers dogmatized it. The expression "from the mouth of the Lord" may thus seem naive and insignificant, but it cannot be dismissed by a refusal to honor the "dictation theory," as all serious and informed scholars must do. The claim that the confession of faith by the individual and by the congregation at baptism represents a word of salvation from God himself merits great consideration and is central to Grundtvig's view of the church. In this confession of faith at baptism, using the words of the Apostles' Creed, which identify the God of our faith and tell the tale of his revelation and continued presence, the Christian congregation responds to God in the covenant terms of his Word. It might be said that in this confession we return God's Word to him with mutual participation in the covenant.

Grundtvig repeatedly says that the signs of the Christian life are the confession of faith, the proclamation of the gospel, and the songs of praise, refusing to include the personal appropriation that was so central for Kierkegaard. Theologians in our own day would probably lift up the proclamation as the primary factor, expressed necessarily and at once in confession of faith and song of praise. The proclamation would be that of the resurrection: God raised Jesus Christ from the dead. In other words, a modern expression of Grundtvig's emphasis would probably be that we base our Christian faith on the *kerygma* of the church.[2]

Besides the three categories of prose writings—the discussion of the Christian life, of the church, and of human living; the sermons; and the educational statements—Grundtvig made a monumental

2. See Reginald Fuller, *The Formation of the Resurrection Narratives* (New York: Macmillan Company, 1971), esp. chap. 8.

contribution to Christian life and worship through his hymns. It was through this creative activity that he renewed the church life of his people. We are including a selection of hymns, songs, and other poetry in translation, and this section will be preceded by an introductory and evaluatory statement.

A final word of caution: Grundtvig should not be "proof-texted." Statements should not be taken out of context and absolutized. This is, of course, true of all writers, but even more so in Grundtvig's case. The reasons are two: Grundtvig expressed himself fervently and even polemically in given situations, and his mind was always in a ferment of further development. He should therefore be read in totality, moving from earlier statements to later ones. An added advantage in reading Grundtvig in totality today, more than a hundred years after his death, lies in the fact that he can be viewed in perspective. Time has not diminished the impact of his ideas, especially when they are related in modern times to the problems of today. A mountain peak is often seen in its greatness at a distance.

WRITINGS ON
THE CHURCH,
CHRISTIAN LIFE,
AND HUMAN LIVING

Translated by
JOHANNES KNUDSEN

The Response of the Church
1825

Una sancta ecclesia perpetuo mansura sit.
[One holy church will be and remain forever.]
—Conf. Aug., art. VII

PREFACE

It should not surprise anyone who has read Professor Clausen's recent book entitled *Catholicism and Protestantism: Their Constitution, Doctrine, and Ritual,*[3] and who takes it seriously, that I confront its author not as a reviewer but as an ecclesiastical opponent.   In this book he has placed himself in the forefront of this country's enemies of the Christian church and scorners of the Word of God.   To be sure, the professor has no recognition as an author, nor, as far as I can see, has he any power of leadership, but his position as a theological professor and his fame as an exegete, among the younger students, give him a churchly predominance in the Danish church which it would be irresponsible to ignore.   In order to indicate this and in order to make clear that my polemics are neither personal nor purely academic but are as purely a church matter as possible, I have called this polemical letter "The Response of the Church."   By this I submit my concern to the judgment of universal Christendom and not merely to the judgment of the literary world.   As a pastor who is an educator in the Christian church, I thus challenge the theological professor, who teaches in the school of the church, and I claim that, as an honest man, he must either make formal apologies to the Christian church for his un-Christian and offensive teachings or

---

3. H. N. Clausen, a newly appointed professor of theology much influenced by Schleiermacher, argued that the understanding of the church should be based on exegesis of the New Testament.   Grundtvig opposed this view on the ground that it bypassed the historic testimony of the church as expressed in the Apostles' Creed.

11

resign his office and discard his Christian name. This is my irrevocable postulate in the name of the Christian church and congregation. In case Professor Clausen refuses to do this, I hereby and in the name of the church, which was and is and shall be, and whose doctrine is clearly known and expressed in history, in the name of the only true, historical-Christian church, declare him to be a false teacher who misuses the Christian name to confuse and seduce the congregation, as far as it is possible for him to do so, and who seeks to undermine the church he professes to serve and affirm.

I would be delighted if my conditional declaration never became effective, but I cannot revoke my contention without excluding myself from the church. The Christian church is no empty or disputable fancy; it is an obvious reality, a well-known historical fact, which can neither be shaken nor destroyed by the protests of the world. What has probably been Christianity from the beginning, this is and will remain Christianity to the end of the world and in all eternity. No one may claim for Christianity what it demonstrably is not and cannot possibly be, for then the true and genuine Christianity would become false, and this is a denial of the truth. This is no idle dispute, for the Christian church is a great and matchless reality. Innumerable events have been occasioned by the church through two thousand years, and it has a monopoly on the witness of these events, good or bad as they may be. This witness it cannot make evident without excluding those who deny it and who wish to gain glory in the realms of ignorance and incomprehension by falsely claiming its name.

The problem is whether or not I, myself, am a false teacher or a blind zealot who postulates uncertainties and ambiguities as the basic teachings of the church or as an attack on these. The answer to this I must leave to the judgment of the church and congregation, even as I place the book of the professor alongside the confession of the church and declare: They cannot possibly be reconciled.

[My action may be regarded as ridiculous] . . . but I am satisfied that I have done my required duty. All reasonable judges will agree that this is a different situation than the many recriminations that have taken place since the Council of Nicaea, when ministers and theologians declared each other to be heretics for their disputable opinions and teachings.   When I was a young man I may have done similar things, but I do not do so now.   When a council, a pope, or a theological faculty usurps the interpretation of the Scriptures and excludes those teachers who interpret differently, without refuting the well-known and original Christianity, the kingdom of God is taken by violence. . . .

Professor of theology H. N. Clausen has in his above-mentioned book expressly and strongly declared that he will tolerate no other source of knowledge and Rule of Faith in the Christian church than the Scriptures.   He has with equal firmness declared that the Scriptures are uncertain and contradictory.   The consequences are undeniably that he rejects the original confession of faith of the Christian church.   He declares the Christianity which has been confessed for centuries to be unknown and unrecognizable.   Inasmuch as he not only claims the Christian name but also claims to be an interpreter of the Scriptures, who teaches others what he himself does not know, namely, what is true Christianity, then he is either deceiving his readers and followers or he is blind to obvious truths. . . .

I know that I will be criticized for my refutation of heresy, for this is what every protest by the church against its false friends is called. But I also know that such a refutation has not been seen for a while, probably not since that book from which I have learned a great deal was written.   It is Irenaeus's blessed book in defense of the church which can be understood and used only now.

Christianshavn, on the Day of Irenaeus 1825

N. F. S. GRUNDTVIG

[MAIN TEXT]

I shall prove that the church promoted by the professor is not the Christian church but a homemade castle in the sky. . . .

Already in the preface the author explains that he has limited his description of Catholicism to the sources given canonicity by the church itself, . . . but that the Protestant church is treated more freely. . . .

The professor justifies this naively by saying that "the Catholic church rests solely on an historical foundation while the Protestant doctrine does not depend on an historical testimony." . . .

He deliberately confuses his own opinion and that of others about the manner in which the protest should have taken place with the actual development of the protest by the Lutheran, the Zwinglian, and the Calvinist congregation through their confessions (symbols) and doctrinal teachings, against the abuse of the papacy. Contrary to Professor Clausen, these did not have any intention of leaving the one, true, universal (Catholic) Christian church, which rests on the foundation of history. . . .

Here we arrive at one of the worst contradictions of the professor. No matter with what dignity he speaks about the Protestant church as one that does not depend on historical testimony and therefore is a church in the sky, and no matter how much he scorns the historical church which remains earthbound until we reach heaven, . . . he still calls his fantasy church by well-known, earthly, historic names, such as Christian and evangelical, and calls upon Christ, the Bible, and Luther. . . .

We will not try to determine whether Professor Clausen knows the true relationship or not, whether he virtually imagines that a church which protests against the faith-confession and history of the Christian church can still be Christian. That his fantasy church neither is nor can be the only, true, well-known or by experience recommended Christian church . . . we can prove. . . .

The name "church," the professor assumes, designates a community for the promotion of universal religiosity.

We shall not quarrel with the professor in the curious discussion of what the name "church" means, but if he claims that the name comes to us as the designation for every community for the promotion of universal religion, he is greatly mistaken. Everyone who is not unfamiliar with church history knows that monastic orders were not called churches, although they undeniably promoted universal religiosity. To avoid unnecessary polemics, however, we shall let the professor believe whatever he wants to about the church, just so that he will admit that the Christian church (*ecclesia Christiana*) is a faith-community with a confession of faith, which is placed before all those who wish to join it. It accepts them by baptism and Communion only when they appropriate the confession. . . . If the professor will not admit this, and if he obstinately insists that his Protestant church, his castle in the sky where everyone may believe what he wants to believe and where the faith-confession contradictorily reads: I believe, I know not what!, is the true Christian church, then we must turn the matter around.   Then we must insist that he admit his error or be declared a liar.   There does exist at the present time a faith-community, calling itself the one, true, Christian church, in which no one is accepted by baptism and Communion without appropriation of the so-called Apostles' Creed.   From this church one excludes himself when he refuses to make the confession, if not to mention when he founds a new church whose members are not bound by faith or knowledge to any confession.   Professor Clausen, who presumably has become a member of this church through baptism and Communion and preceding confession, has by the current book undeniably excluded himself.   When he nevertheless claims to be a member of the Christian church, he must prove that the faith-fellowship, to which he scornfully turns his back, has falsely appropriated and borne the name of the Christian church. If he does not do this he must allow himself to be declared a member of the heretical community outside the church, which has only the belief in common that the church has gone astray and that their protest is sufficient to disgrace and condemn it. . . .

After the professor has interred Catholicism which, according to his own explanation, is the historical-Christian and therefore the one true Christian church, he introduces a brand new concept which he calls the Protestant church, the church of contradiction.   According to his account, and he is certainly the best judge of his own imaginary creation, it starts out from the same dogmatic assumption as the Catholic, historic-Christian church.   This is faith in the revelation in Jesus Christ.   It diverges from this immediately, however, and makes a critical distinction between the written word and the oral tradition.   It is to be admitted, he says, that Christianity has been transmitted by oral instruction before the Scriptures were written and that most of the Sacred Scriptures are fruits of the oldest Christian tradition. The possibility could not be rejected that a number of statements by Jesus and the apostles may have been preserved in the writings of the fathers so that they might be read in

their pristine purity. . . . Nevertheless, even though it was possible
that a doctrine, bypassed in Scripture, was traced back to Jesus or
the apostles, it would not be justified to equate this with those of
Sacred Scripture. . . .

In other words, in the Protestant church of the professor the
written word is everything and even a word from the mouth of Jesus
could not change it a whit. . . .

We read further that the written word is the only form in which
the doctrine has maintained a demonstrable integrity. . . . Scripture is the complete and adequate vehicle for doctrine. Nothing can
be added and nothing can be taken away. Scripture is its own
interpreter, clear and obvious to every seeing eye. . . . Turning the
pages, however, . . . we hear that the Protestant who works with
Scripture cannot conceal the fact that repetitions which should have
been avoided are just as frequent as omissions which should have
been filled. Scripture is often silent where we wish it to speak. It
is vague and obscure where the eye yearns for a guiding light. . . .

This should be adequate proof of how the professor, with a terri-
ble superstition, seeks to reconcile contradictions in his Protestant
church. It is also sufficient to remove any desire to belong to it. It
proves that it was not this church which the Reformers sought to
illuminate by Scripture. There is even more to it. On the following page we read that no word has come to us from Jesus himself and
that no word is expressly sealed by his highest authority. The
teachings and deeds of Jesus have not been registered in a complete
and continuous account. Two of his biographers were not even
apostolic eyewitnesses. The four Gospels can be chronologically
harmonized only with difficulty and there are open differences and
contradictions. The predominantly dogmatic part of our Sacred
Scriptures has been authored by that apostle who had neither seen
the Lord and Master with his own eyes or heard him with his own
ears. Dogmatics and ethics are mixed up, as are essentials and
allegorical nonessentials, literalism and imagery, the universal and
the temporal, the Christian and the Hebraic. The individuality of
the apostles is undeniably evident in the treatment of the Christian
doctrines. This illustrates the theological variety that has characterized the Christian church ever since, so that only those of

philological learning and philosophical criticism can fill in the loopholes, explain the ambiguities, and firm up all the vagueness. Finally, the authenticity of several of the books can only be approximated, inasmuch as the text has undergone the fate of all other books.   Biblical criticism and hermeneutics show us problems which will forever lead to polemics in the Christian world.

All readers must therefore be convinced that the Protestant church, with which Professor Clausen is pregnant, is a curious castle in the sky.   There has never been a more foolish belief in the whole world than the insistence that a book at one time can be a source of information and Rule of Faith for its readers and at the same time be their dust-rag. . . .

This, then, is supposed to be the divine ideal at which the Christian church under the guidance of God has arrived and has now fulfilled in the mind of Professor Clausen. . . . But this means that truth and falsehood about the relationship of God and man are equally biblical, equally Christian.   It follows that the Bible and Christianity are not a true and divine revelation but a false and demonic one. . . .

We now understand the wise judgment of the Christian church, which has been, is, and ever shall be, that all those who are to be baptized are asked: Do you renounce the devil and all his works and all his ways? . . .

It is therefore obvious that the Christianity of Professor Clausen is completely false.   His Protestant church is a temple for an idol in which falsehood is proclaimed as truth. . . . It is likewise certain that Professor Clausen baselessly calls the church he wishes to found a biblical and Christian church.   He contradicts the words of the Bible and he finds no Rule of Faith in it.   On the contrary, he questions the genuine character of the New Testament, saying that the text is uncertain and that interpretation is a bone of contention.

The question remains, then, whether the historic-Christian church, into which we enter through baptism and Communion, has a better claim upon the Christian name. . . .

The peculiar characteristics upon which the oldest Christian church was founded and by which it was recognizable by its enemies but most of all by its friends must be found in every church with the

justified claim of being Christian. This, I insist, will be found in
our church and will be found wherever the apostolic Confession of
Faith is made the exclusive condition for admission into the community, and where the means of grace, baptism and Communion,
are taken to have a similar salutary power as the Confession of
Faith. . . .

Thus, we meet Professor Clausen and all those who make revela-
tory claims for their own dreams and intellectual concoctions with
the unshakable fact that there has been and is now one Christianity
on earth, distinguished from everything else by its matchless Confession of Faith. On all tongues and in many and marvelous ways it
has proclaimed and does yet proclaim faith in Jesus Christ, the
crucified and arisen, as the certain and only way to salvation for
sinners, a way that leads through baptism and Communion to the
kingdom of God and the land of the living. . . .

The means of grace and the corresponding Confession of Faith are
the only features which all Christians, in all situations, in all congregations, and at all times have had in common. This has identified the Christian church for its friends and enemies and united the
congregation. . . .

[After a survey of historical testimony, Grundtvig writes about
the Reformers.]

It is a certainty that whatever the Reformers, with Martin Luther
at their head, in their conflict with the pope as theologians have
postulated about Scriptures as the Rule of Faith, they always presupposed as ministers, i.e., as teachers in the church, the church and
its faith. They agreed that Scripture could be rightly interpreted
only by the aid of the Holy Spirit. . . . It is also a certainty that
our church, in the Augsburg Confession, against which neither
Luther nor Melanchthon protested, bound its teachers to the Apostolic Confession of Faith (Art. III) and to the one, true, historical-
Christian, unchangeable Catholic church (Arts. VII and XXI). It is
finally certain that no one elevated the simple childhood faith above
all education more than Martin Luther. He could not show his
reliance upon the foundation of the church more clearly than by
tying the apostolic confession inseparably to baptism and by placing

it in the Small Catechism as the basis for childhood faith and childhood teaching.

If we concede to Professor Clausen, we must necessarily admit
that all the Reformers were in error concerning the original shape of
the Christian church and that they, knowingly or unknowingly, laid
the foundation for the new *exegetical papacy,* under whose rule the
entire Christian church is groaning.   All Christian scholars must
unite to destroy this at the roots.   We have now reached the point
where the youngest professor at our academy attempts, as *summus
theologus,* to be the exegetical pope of the church.   At his command
the historic-Christian church is to be demolished and a new one is to
be built from theological wastepaper.

Introduction to Nordic Mythology
1832

Yes, ye sons of heroic men,
Let us consider our rightful gain!
Each man different from the rest,
Freedom will always serve us best,
Freedom, not as by fire and flood,
Sickness, hunger and ill-shed blood,
Freedom, not as for beasts of prey,
But for adults in the light of day,
Rhyming with reason to take a stand
In our illusory fantasy-land.

. . . .

Freedom must be our great Nordic claim,
Loki and Thor, both must share the same.
Freedom's flag for the Word unfurled
In its newly created world.

. . . .

Freedom for all that is spirit-born,
Deeply resentful of shackles worn.

INTRODUCTION

1. Universal-Historic Scholarship[4]

[Grundtvig begins his introduction by postulating that clarity, while it may be the goal of spiritual endeavor, cannot also be the guidance toward this goal. It is not true that clarity is the birthmark of light and that practicality is the mark of truth. Should this viewpoint obtain, we would have only an appearance of perfection; we will not have reached the goal. The Italian (Roman or Renaissance) scholarship of perfection was thus a pseudo-concept which had shadowy, spiritual results. Consequently, it faded away in the

---

4. The Danish word *"Vidskab,"* which can also mean "science" or "knowledge," is translated throughout this essay as "scholarship."

eighteenth century, even as it prevailed in the academic life of England. It cannot be resurrected, for it was inimical toward a real spiritual life, toward a living, encompassing culture and a scholarship of the people, which should prevail in the North as the continuation of its ancient heritage.]

I insist that when we consider the world of the spirit with Nordic eyes and in the light of Christianity, we arrive at a concept of a universal-historic development, art, and scholarship which encompasses all of human living. With all its dynamics, its conditions, and its consequences, the world of the spirit liberates, strengthens, and enlivens all that is in accord with the welfare of the individual, the peoples, and all of humanity. It will lead us to the most perfect explication of life possible on this earth. It is this Graeco-Nordic or neo-Danish growth and spiritual formation which gives the myths of the North their universal-historic significance, for they contain its seed. All this has inestimable value for us, and it is this scholarship which I desire to describe—from its own inner worth as well as in contrast to the Roman-Italian plague and destruction. . . .

When I speak of a neo-Danish growth, I am not using the term "Danish" in its narrow sense, as I often do in an appreciative manner. I use it with its Old-Norse coverage, when it encompassed the area from the Eider River to Tromsø, from the North Sea to Finland, and even reached the Nordic emigrés on the Isle of Hercules. Furthermore, when I speak of the revival of a Christian and an Old-Danish scholarship, I am not speaking of two segments which only a poet could unify. Nor am I speaking of something Christian bound to the Christian faith. I am speaking of a Graeco-Nordic growth which has a living and a universally-historic character by the aid of a basic Mosaic-Christian "Anskuelse."[5]

5. The term "Anskuelse" is a key term in the argument of this essay. It means "idea," "philosophy," "point of view," but none of these terms represents the meaning accurately. The term is akin to the German "Anschauung," and it indicates an explanation or application. Grundtvig took it over from Schelling. It is therefore to be distinguished from faith as well as doctrine. Doctrine is an explication of the faith itself, but "Anskuelse" is the attitude toward and the explanation of the world in which the faith lives. "Anskuelse" is a derivative from the faith and it can be altered and adjusted to changing circumstances without jeopardy to the faith. During the essay Grundtvig makes the point that a Christian may change his "Anskuelse" with equanimity, while a "naturalist" cannot give up his "Anskuelse," for this is his only possession. Because the term is so essential to Grundtvig's argument and because the use of either "idea," "philosophy," or "point of view" brings connotations extraneous to the argument, we have chosen to use the original Danish term in quotation marks, hoping that this explanation may make clear what is meant.

No matter if one is a Christian or a heathen (naturalist), one could not possibly be an historian with any spiritual insight if one did not immediately realize that it was neither Scythians nor barbarians which so wonderfully shattered the shackles of mankind in the days of Rome. It was the higher Christian *"Anskuelse,"* and it was the same *"Anskuelse,"* which gave the Roman pope his deathblow when it was revived by Luther. It is this and this alone which has endowed the habits of thought, the culture, and the scholarship of the new world, the world of the people, with their universally human character, for this was missing in the old world, although the misdeeds of Rome had not erased it. A spiritless and lifeless scholarship, which knows no other explanation than dissolution and which takes pride in its ability to reduce all spirituality to hot air and to partition divinity into the four elements, a scholarship such as the Roman-Italian, which raves about the Golden Age of Augustus as wolves rave about a famine and worms about pestilence, such a scholarship must necessarily regard Christianity as a catastrophe which disrupted the Roman enlightenment and happiness. No wonder the Romans traced the surprising consequences of Christianity to revery and fanaticism, lies and superstitions, which they gave polite names out of urbanity. But one need not be a monkey or a Roman just because one is a heathen. This has been proved by the history and poetry of Greece and the ancient North. If one is a real person, who knows himself to be different from the dumb creatures and to be related to the immortal gods, addressed by the spirit of God and man in all tongues known to man, then one bows down to that spirit, which was given voice on the glowing lips of the apostles in living words from Jerusalem. That spirit performed wonders for human welfare to the ends of the world; it opens the eyes of men to perceive the wonderful path of the children of heaven and earth; it reveals a friendly perspective across the Sea of Death to the Land of the Living, the eternal kingdom of the Father.

Be he a Christian or a heathen, a Turk or a Jew, every person who is conscious of his spiritual nature is in himself a marvelous enigma; he will reject nothing merely because it is wondrous and apparently as much without explanation as he is himself. On the contrary, wonder attracts him in an irresistible manner because he sees his image reflected, and he hopes to find the solution to his own enigma. He knows that he cannot find his answers in situations where comprehension is apparent. Such a person, whether he be of one faith or another, or even of no faith in divinity whatsoever, will not be attracted to educated people whose wisdom is so apparent that it can be appropriated in an hour of memorization or even taught to smart dogs. He is attracted to the dim and profound natures whose thought is profound and intuitive, whose emotions run deeper than any probe, and whose enthusiasm carries beyond themselves. Such persons who defy the Roman enlightenment are yet plentiful in our Nordic countries. As lecturer and author I have met a good many.

I am confident that when the North awakens, as it must, many will hearken to the thought that the Mosaic-Christian *"Anskuelse,"* whether it be poetic or historic, whether it has a natural or a supernatural origin, is the only true, basic *"Anskuelse"* of human living. It manifested itself when all the pagan gods were dead, when all spirit had disappeared, and when eternity was an empty word. By its unmatched and blessed consequences through eighteen centuries it has vouched for its own divine origin as well as for the divinity of Christ. This *"Anskuelse"* must therefore be our guiding star for science as well as for practical living. Before this can happen, however, we must recognize the difference not only between Christianity and Bible-faith but also between the Christian faith and the Christian *"Anskuelse."* This will take some doing, but the evidence is so strong that recognition is inevitable.

All enlightened people in the serious-minded and historic North must necessarily soon recognize that the point of disagreement between Christians and the naturalists is not the divinity of Christ or the divinity of the Christian *"Anskuelse."* This has been demonstrated unshakably through eighteen centuries. The dispute is elsewhere. Theologically the dispute might be said to be the question of Christ's eternal divinity, but historically it is clearly expressed in conflicting views of natural man. All people of the spirit can agree that natural man is created in the image of God and that God's living breath gave him all that was necessary to fulfill his purpose as a Son of God. That natural man also suffered an early

accident which threw earth out of balance with heaven, pushed time
out of relation to eternity, and brought confusion to the nature of
man is attested to by daily and universal-historic experience to such
a degree that it cannot be denied by a person with a trace of spirit
and a spark of the love for truth. The main question is not even the
name to give to this accident. Naturalists do not like to call it "The
Fall"; it sounds trivial to them. They would rather say "error" or
"aberration." But even the naturalists realize that it can be called
both and that a deviation from a natural course must be sinful and
thus lead to a fall. They agree therefore that semantics are not
worth a dispute. The problem is not the name but whether the
damage can be repaired in a natural way.

This is our great ecclesiastical dispute, and all compromise is out
of the question. There is no middle way other than a paralyzing
doubt which either gives way to faith or paralyzes all action so that
we are thrown into the bottomless pit of contradictions. The latter
is an eternal death and hell for the spirit. When we, however,
acknowledge our conflict and strive, each in his own church community, to live strictly by it, then we will no longer hesitate to share
"Anskuelse" in the matters that are evident in both situations. Only
then will experience prove whether the Christians or the naturalists
are wrong. By the fruits we can know the tree. As long, however,
as we confuse our church communities, the result is chaos and bitter
strife is inevitable. Christians believe that human nature was so
corrupted by the Fall that all remedy is out of the question. They
hold up baptism as a bath of reconciliation in which the faithful are
spiritually re-created. The common and individual task in the
church is to nurture the new being into a divine union with the
God-man and savior, Jesus Christ. This cannot be accepted without contradiction by the naturalist. He must declare this faith to be
a coarse misunderstanding. He must maintain that although this
does not ruin the divine fruits of the Christian *"Anskuelse,"* it must
surely weaken them and prevent the explanation. He must insist
that the old nature can and must be remedied, but he must deny the
Christian claim that we must be received into Christ. Rather, he
must claim that we must receive him as a divine example of what we
are to attain by purification: children of men who raise themselves to

be children of God. Spiritual people will immediately perceive how discriminating this contradiction is, but they will also realize that it is no more challenging to our historic *"Anskuelse"* of Christianity than opposing theories of astronomy would be to our view of the heavens. In both cases the same phenomena are approached in a different manner. Whether or not we believe in a geocentric or a heliocentric view of the universe, only a fool would maintain that the earth is the source of its own light or that days may pass by without a relationship of earth and sun. Spiritually speaking: Either the Son of God becomes the son of man or the son of man becomes the Son of God!

Only when we realize this, so that we meet each other as Chaldeans or Copernicans in the world of the spirit, not disagreeing about the world, merely about its laws, only then can we cooperate as teachers without a battle of books. With this understanding, however, we can cooperate, realizing that if the books are to decide the differences they must be genuinely inspired. The matter is not solved by books but by an explanation of human living. Books cannot settle issues; they can only describe. If we blame the books, life is not changed, only misused. . . .

We must realize that learning is one matter, culture and competence for living as human beings and citizens is another. Both can be combined, although hardly by the masses, and they must not oppose one another. They must be separate in order not to seek to suppress, confuse, or corrupt one another.

Culture and competence must always be relevant to the momentary life of the people; learning must be relevant to the total life of mankind. When learning is genuine, it encompasses culture and competence, but the latter can only encompass learning in an intuitive sort of way. Learning will be misleading, particularly among educators, if it is not juxtaposed by the culture of a people, which compels learning to recognize the life here and now; the culture of a people will become superficial if it is not kept alive by learning. . . . Wise educational institutions must therefore be gauged to progressive enlightenment and culture. If we are vain enough to shape our children and our descendants as a full-blown lithograph of ourselves, we bring shame upon ourselves and we help to make the coming generations unhappy. Man is not a monkey destined to imitate other animals or, eventually, to imitate himself. He is a marvelous and wondrous creature in whom divine forces are proclaimed, evolved, and clarified through thousands of generations. He is a divine experiment, which demonstrates how spirit and dust can interpenetrate one another and be transfigured in a common, divine consciousness. In this manner man must be regarded, if we are to have spiritual scholarship on earth, and thus is man regarded wherever the Mosaic-Christian *"Anskuelse"* has been the inspiration.

The history of this *"Anskuelse"* proves that it is not an empty fantasy and that it is not alien to man. To the degree that it was appropriated, life maintained a natural pattern, performing in a wondrous, glorious, and blessed way. Academically this *"Anskuelse"* has never prevailed, because ancient Roman scholarship, as well as its Italian phantom, were lifeless. They proceeded from the written letter rather than the living word, and the ironclad necessity became death, not life. They led man to the grave rather than to heaven, even directing him back through animal stages to the worms rather than to the creator via the ladder of the spirit. The Old-Norse scholarship made a faint attempt, in England and in Iceland, to ally itself with heaven and with the life of the people, but the efforts were fragmentary and the time had not yet arrived for the scholarship of the Northmen. The effort was pleasing, and in its unpredictable consequences it delayed death. It had to fail, but now the time has come. We have the need and we have the means; all we want now is the willpower. The great book of experience has been opened to guide us past the rocks and the maelstroms which lead to destruction. We can now survive the great storms of the ocean. It is foolishness to attempt to make all people equally wise. If we tried to do this, we would only make everyone equally stupid. But to promote a basically uniform enlightenment in all classes of people and to open all careers to constant progress, this, like everything that leads to the free and orderly development of life forces, is not only wise but absolutely necessary if peoples and states are to prosper.

What all countries need is a *civic and noble academy* or, in other words, a higher institute for the culture of the people and for practi-

cal competence in all major subjects.   This need must be met, and
soon, for the sake of society as well as for the sake of learning. . . .

Such an institution must grow out of learning and it must have a
living relationship to knowledge in order not to be hostile or static.
Such an institution must be independent, however, so as not to
become a tail or a shadow.   It has to be a real, spiritual force by
which life and the moment manifest their inalienable rights, often
unappreciated by the wise.   The land of our fathers, in its natural
and historic character, will thus be related to the life of reality and
the requirements of the moment.   This will be the common core
from which the institution will branch out into all major functions
of everyday life, combining all civic efforts.   In this academy all the
civil servants of the state who do not need academic learning but
who do need life, perspective, and practical competence, and all
those who wish to share a life of culture, will have a desired opportunity to develop practically and to get to know one another.   Here
also the literature of our country will become useful, and that literature will find the encouragement without which it will soon be a
dying show-flower.   When enlightenment is made fruitful for the
people, the life of the people will, in turn, fructify scholarship. . . .

2. Myths and Mythologies

I need hardly inform the reader about the common difference
between myths and mythologies.   Anyone can read a score of the
latter without meeting a single myth.   During the past five hundred
years there has existed a kind of freemasonry in the republic of the
learned by which nothing under heaven or on earth was concealed for
ourselves.   For the lay reader, however, the subject of our discussion
was to be completely esoteric.   When we wrote histories, we re-
corded names and dates for our own convenience, and we explained
the relationship of events about which the reader was kept in the
dark.   When we wrote mythologies, we assumed that the reader
either knew all the details of the myths or that he did not care about
them.   We assumed that he was interested in our own ingenious
fancies in regard to ancient follies, which were best forgotten save as
subjects for our fantasizing.

The difference between myths and mythologies is quite inciden-

tal, but it is essential.   Mythologies are books and myths were not.
As their name implies, myths were living, oral words.   They did
not employ ordinary language but a language of imagery.   The
ancients were serious when they called this the language of the gods,
and this is what we still call it poetically, albeit with tongue in
cheek.   I am not sure that the reader will appreciate the essential
difference nor the incidental.   I have already sought to emphasize
the enormous difference between word and script, given equal circumstances, but because the difference is so enormous, as it also is
between life and death, I must expect that my dead, written proof of
the advantages of the living word has prevailed very little against the
constant oral assurance that the dead letters have unbelievable advantages.   I must therefore renew my efforts to roll the rock of
Sisyphus and beg the reader to consider the undeniable philosophical
truth that life is not propagated by the dead but by the living.   Life
profits as little by dead words as by dead fish; as little by blunt quills
as by pointed pens of steel; as little by shadowy words as by shadowy
people.   When the naked truth does not kill the faith in letters, it is
only because you cannot rekill a dead person, as the poet[6] said; it is
even more because the truth in this case is itself a dead letter.   The
truth cannot speak for itself but must wait for the contradiction to
refute itself.   Should the reader, however, by a stroke of good
fortune discover the secret, which Latins conceal but which we reveal
everytime we open our mouth, namely, that the word belongs in
the mouth and not in the pen and that ideas and emotions, faith and
"Anskuelse" are expressed orally, not manually, and in brief and
precise, clear and living, expressive, informative, and propagating
manner, should the reader have taken this giant step out of the
grave, then he would see immediately and without my prodding
what a wonderful light is shed upon our human living.   This is no
miracle; it simply demonstrates how differently we regard things
when we are under the open skies rather than in a casket in a tomb or
sit by a dim reading lamp, surrounded by human skulls.   If the
reader is still in this grave, neither my book nor all the books in the
world can teach him to appreciate the living word.   All I dare hope

6. Jens Baggesen.

is that those who can neither read nor write may profit from the word by hearing and speaking it. Children are born with a tongue and with ears but not with books under their arms or with a pen in their hand. We may well wonder what people wrote before someone started to speak. . . .

When, therefore, I try to write tolerably about the myths, I must presume that the reader knows what an inspired word can mean in its full power. Originally the myths were such words everywhere, or, to avoid argument, at any rate in Greece and in the North. We plainly see that in both places poetry is older than prose. The same is true in the later literature of Italy, France, Spain, England, Germany, and the North. It is therefore incomprehensible how the desperate idea arose that man's thought originally was prosaic—even a large and self-conscious toad can be prosaic—and that it then rose as a caterpillar ascends to become a beautifully winged butterfly. It would be incomprehensible, I say, how the idea arose in defiance of man's natural laws and the clear testimony of history, if we had not been familiar with the dark school,[7] where the caterpillar was really hatched in an Egyptian manner to become a curious butterfly, which was praised for its unnatural birth and was elevated above all the birds of the forest that sing in a natural manner.

Yes, in Rome, among the robbers, things took place much as among decent people, and when Roman history now is taken to be a divine and natural revelation by the last five hundred years of the dark school, even though it is distorted, blindly accepted, and unspiritually interpreted, then we begin to understand what it is all about. . . .

Although the Romans obviously were the most unpoetic of all the famous peoples in ancient times, and although they were an artificial people[8] from the beginning, furthering their own goal, which was the suppression of all natural peoples, we can still trace that development in their history which is characteristic for human nature and which cannot be disturbed, only corrupted. Even the Romans

7. Grundtvig's expression for self-centered, world-removed academia was "black school."

8. Grundtvig speaks of a "natural people," which is indigenous to its territory and situation, and of an "artificial people," created by an idea, an opportunity, or a task, such as the Roman people, or by divine guidance, such as the Hebrew people.

had their age of imagination under the seven kings, then an age of
emotion in the brilliant days of the Republic, and then an age of
reason from the time of Cato the Elder.   The difference is that from
the beginning everything Roman had a secular, common, and mis-
anthropic tendency, so that their most profound and poetic myth is
the one about Mars and the wolverine,[9] in which all of Roman
history is mirrored. . . .

Turning now to the Hebrews, the most poetic of all ancient
peoples, we see that although they were an artificial people, they
were a genuine people which has a written history from the beginning of its lifetime.   It also has a book of laws with the universal-
historic introduction which justifiably is called "Genesis" or "The
Mother."   Its growth is naturally the same.   First an age of imagination up to Moses, then an age of emotion and action up to Solomon, and then the age of reason.

No matter how eagerly the theologians of the Reformation period
tried to praise the Hebrew language as the basic language and the
Mosaic laws as the model constitution, they never considered the
Hebrew people to be the normative people, which would have been
overmuch wiser.   They could then have arranged and evaluated
ancient history and Roman literature accordingly.   For the supernatural and the unnatural became synonymous for them, and while
they snorted against all paganism as pure idolatry, they idolized the
Roman werewolf and fostered it as a Capitoline Jupiter in the world
of the spirit. . . .   So even though the living word was awakened in
and through Martin Luther to prove that the Spirit, which performs
mighty deeds, lives not in scriptures but in the Word, lives not in a
paper house or in a fancy structure built of mortar and stone, lives
not in houses built with hands, even then in the days of Luther the
alphabetic letters were idolized, although it was well known that the
Bible had not performed heroic deeds, at least not in Latin, but that
it had patiently permitted itself to be misused by popes and
clerics. . . .

We must realize now that in order to understand the growth of
man in history we must have a wide, even colossal, perspective,

9. Romulus, the legendary founder of Rome, allegedly was the offspring of Mars, the god of
war, and a wolf.

where a little more or less makes no difference. Relatively speaking, who can doubt that ancient history was the age of imagination, the Middle Ages the age of emotion, and modern times the age of reason. Ancient literature is the most poetic; that of the Middle Ages is the most historic; and that of modern times is the most philosophical. If we compare this with our daily experience, we will see that, relatively speaking, imagination is dominant in youth, emotion in adulthood, and reason in old age. . . .

If the modern era, which has taken upon itself the task of understanding the old, had had a scholarly spirit, it would have saved both of the artificial peoples (the Hebrew and the Roman) to the last, and it would have concentrated its attention upon the Greeks as the only one of the natural peoples that was known through a complete developmental period, namely, the five centuries from Solon to Christ and Augustus. The modern era would soon have discovered that, relatively speaking, the whole period before Solon was the age of imagination, that emotions ruled from him to Alexander, and that reason, as it was, took over with the library at Alexandria and its high school of learning. . . .

[Grundtvig now argues that all the ancient peoples fell into the error of relying on a written rationalization of their values.]

Even the Christian church, though created by inspiration, was reduced to relying on the letter. This should have been recognized and the scholars of our day should have asked if there had not been an oral world even in Israel which was propagated from generation to generation as a living source for spiritual rebirth. They would soon have discovered . . . that the Ten Commandments and the farewell address of Moses [Exod. 19, 20; Deut. 31, 32] were two living words which were to be transmitted orally in all people and as a matter of course by the pious. By this the unity of the *"Anskuelse"* was maintained and life was perpetuated, even privately, when it seemed to have disappeared.

If this little, divine word, which, by divine power, maintained and gave new birth to the life of Israel even though it took place in the order of nature, had been discovered, then the corresponding word would have been found in the Christian church. It would have been obvious, for it is solemnly propagated at both sacraments.

In the confession of faith at baptism it gives brief and clear expression to all of the basic Christian *"Anskuelse"*: of the creator of the world as a Father who clearly revealed to his erring children his love in the God-man, Jesus Christ, his only-begotten Son, and whose Holy Spirit creates out of those who believe, a holy fellowship and a holy people who have the forgiveness of sins and who are to inherit eternal life!

That the Christian *"Anskuelse"* was reborn in the days of Luther by this little word, in full accord with the New Testament, is undoubtedly a great wonder, but like all divine wonders it is in the order of nature. Without a living word it would have been unnatural sorcery, unworthy of God, and, in fact, impossible.

If we have now arrived at that insight which our fathers lacked so that we begin to understand the life of man in great perspective, we will acquire, as a main result, a light and living concept of spirit as the higher force of life. This concept is not airy or confused, and it has a corresponding expression in a spoken word, which is its earthly home. . . .

At this stage we discover that it was not only a spiritual confusion in the minds of people, when they sired the irresponsible eulogies on the written word. They did not realize that this was only a pictorial expression which can be misused. Contrariwise, we are to realize that we must grasp the invisible and winged word before we can write it down. We shall be disillusioned if we imagine that we have a forceful word when we have only its shadow through a pen. . . .

But then we must ask: Why do we need myths when we have the Christian *"Anskuelse"*? Why clouds and stars, when we have the sun and the moon?

First of all, I must remark that if the myths of Greece and the North were not necessary we would yet need to understand them more than anything else. Their influence has been universally historic, and their literatures are the only original ones. Their languages were indispensable. But I will answer the question as best I can. In regard to the clouds, even the sun would not do without them, as long as it is to shed its light over the earth; and the moon would want the stars, especially the Pleiades and the Big Dipper. In other words: Christianity has no other imagery than the marvelous parables of the Lord and that which arose out of his earthly life. All this, however, belongs to the church and to its school, and it applies only to the way to eternal life. We, however, have a temporal career, which must be considered in a spiritual light. Our soul as well as our body has temporal needs, and our creator wants us to work for these by the light and the power he has given us. He gave manna to his people in the desert, but he does not feed us in a land where we can sow and reap. The imagery of the Old Testament is undoubtedly accurate and encompassing enough for us to use, and if we could appropriate it the sun would rise in the land of cognition, but it will be too profound and it will be scholarly unusable as long as Hebrew is a dead language. I am not in doubt that the time will soon be here when the remnant of this remarkable people and its language will be resurrected as Lazarus was, but this must take place, as must everything related to this people, in a wondrous way not yet apparent. . . . So much is clear, however, the emphasis is now on the imagery of Greece and the North. By enlivening our knowledge of man and by beautifying our existence they will earn our gratitude and bring us far toward our goal of understanding.

Assuming that the myths of every people are a pleasing expression of its spirit and that they form its spiritual temple, they are necessarily prophetic. They forebode the destiny of a people. This happens in the sense that the youth of every person, and especially that of poets, is prophetic. No one can rise above the spiritual promises contained in the dreams and the desires of his youth. We can thus know beforehand that the youthful dreams of the Greeks and the Northmen must have a depth and a scope far beyond the notions of mythologists who make them an expression of everyday life. . . .

The reader will agree with me that the Greeks reached further in their youthful imaginings than they did even in the art and scholarship of their maturity. It must have been a great joy to hear the mouth harp improvisations of the great-grandparents of Homer as their eyes glowed with the promises of the future. From this we can learn how to go beyond the Greeks in arts and sciences, if we only have the greater desire, the deeper commitment, and the stronger assistance which they lacked.

Contrary to the backward postulates of the dark school, it is not in the nature of imagination to fail to develop a reality corresponding to imagination.   The cause for the failure must lie in the mishap which happened to human nature and disturbed its original condition.   Daily experience as well as universal-historic experience teach us that the laws of the spirit are much like atmospheric laws. Imagination influences emotions in a manner corresponding to its height so that the column will rise in the tube of reason to its original height.   If we have the idea of a beautiful structure built by mortar and stone, sounds or ideas, it will influence us so that we attack our project and complete it.   It will then be an accurate replica of the idea.   It is thus a contradiction to assume that a creature can be inspired toward heaven and end by burrowing into the ground in order to prove himself.

If we have appropriated the Christian *"Anskuelse"* of man, we will know that imagination was not perfect after the Fall, as little as any other human quality.   Imagination's fault, however, was not that it soared too high, for that which, like the spirit of God, descended from heaven must ascend again; its fault was that it did not fly high enough.   It remained on the ground or it got lost among the stars. Hence the idolatry.   When those who are self-opinionated scold imagination for its excesses and counsel it to stay close to the ground, the old Adam can claim his innocence.   He will drown in the water he uses to wash his hands, even as he roguishly laments that this philosophy is too deep for him.

When imagination is spiritual, it may justifiably claim a relative innocence, for it is the creator of poetry.   Any poet would wish that his life was an expression of his inspiration; any people would want to give expression to the inspiration of its poets.

The fault is found where we least desire it, in the heart, as the Mosaic-Christian *"Anskuelse"* has shown beyond any doubt.   If the heart had not been damaged, the Israelites, and especially the Christians, would have been demigods.   When the heart was not profound, action and reason suffered.   Reason is but a clarified emotion, and it becomes clarified when it determines an action, which reveals its nature.   This demonstrates that reason arises gradually out of experience and it teaches us to understand human living only by a consideration of history. The speculation that does not learn from life becomes a changeling on whom, as we know from our nursery days, baptism and Christianity make no impression and all careful nurture is wasted.

It was not a fault of the Greeks that they started to sing about the presence of the gods, for man is created in the image of God so as to be like unto him. He who wishes to ascend to the immortal gods must hear their songs in the cradle; he must visualize them as images and models for what he is to become. The fault was not that the gods were anthropomorphized. It lay in the fact that the gods were false. They were but shadows of the divinity in man, and therefore they could not ascend spiritually. Or they could be imitated in a mediocre manner, so that action sank far below the idea. The sons of the gods misbehaved; they could not reach heaven. Like demigods they were suspended with Pegasus or plunged like Phaethon.

When the divine resemblance and the heavenly ascent failed so miserably, the explanation cannot be a divine consciousness but a misunderstanding of spirituality, as if the myths were empty and painted boxes which were either discarded or inadequately ballasted. This is what happened in Greece, for the gods and demigods were dead even in the days of Solon. Gods and their imagery are dead when the masses bow down to idols, even as the learned ones ridicule them or make games with them. Under these circumstances the awakening which was attempted by the dramatic poets had to fail. These did not become heralds of a spiritual scholarship but *coryphaei*[10] at the funeral of poetry. Even Athens did not rise much higher, although Plato has shed immortal glory upon Greek scholarship. He deserves to be called divine when he, with great talent, sought to establish the link between heaven and earth, between man and the immortal gods.

The Greeks progressed no further. They worshiped Plato but they followed Aristotle, and mankind has never proceeded beyond this. We can go even further, however. We know that the ascension succeeded in Palestine, and with the Christian *"Anskuelse"* we

10. Chorus leaders.

may learn to understand it as the temporal goal of mankind, whatever happens to the real imitation that leads to eternal life.

Again I must call attention to the peculiar difference between Christians and the naturalists who share the Christian *"Anskuelse."* When we share the *"Anskuelse"* and promote it, instead of fighting and deviling about it, as we have done up to now, we become aware of the difference at all main points. As old-time Christians we believe, and must continue to believe, that Christ really ascended into heaven for us and, in a manner of speaking, with us, so that we shall follow him. We believe this whether we understand it or not. But the naturalist is convinced, and has to be convinced, that Christ ascended to heaven as a witness to the possibility and as an example for us. They claim that we must understand the ascension and only then imitate it. This difference does not mean that we must scorn scholarship nor that the naturalist must be more concerned about a spiritual scholarship, which can explain life, than we have to be. For us the understanding is a temporal concern, for him it is a salutary matter.

Folk-Life[11] and Christianity
October 17, 1847

"Following their master's example, the Grundtvigians mix up Danishness, Nordicness, and Scandinavianism with Christianity. They toy with folk-life and nationalism in an alarming manner, especially when they include the sacred life."

This curious item in the *Berlingske* daily concerning a sect of which I am allegedly the head, if we are to believe the name, would have been amusing if I had not known that many others than the modest vicar[12] sit in judgment on bishops and professors, even as they do on the minister at Vartov.[13] They are suspicious of my so-called confusion of Danishness and Christianity. Because I know this, and also because I know that there is need for information about both realms, the item in the paper reminded me that I who am best equipped to give this information probably have neglected to do this as well as I might. I deliberately mention only Danishness and Christianity, for I know that I have never related Nordicness, let alone the Mesopotamian Scandinavianism, to Christianity in such a manner that even the cataracted vicar could imagine that I

---

11. The Danish words *"folkelighed,"* a noun, and *"folkelig,"* an adjective, do not have adequate equivalents in the English language. To be sure, we have the term "folk" as used in "folk songs" and "folk dances," etc., and this does represent something of the Danish intent, having reference to the common people in contrast to the sophisticated intelligentsia. But the Danish term also expresses the totality of a country's population. For this we use the term "people" in English. It seems a bit awkward to use two terms in the translation and even more awkward to use the Danish term in quotes. We shall therefore translate the noun *"folkelighed"* by the term "folk-life," meaning the life of a people in a certain country. The adjective *"folkelig"* we shall translate in a variety of ways. Always, however, the concept of a total people must be included in the understanding.
12. The author of the article to which Grundtvig responds signed himself "A Rural Vicar."
13. Grundtvig was the pastor of the chapel at Vartov, a home for the aged in Copenhagen. He preached regularly from the chapel pulpit from 1839 to 1872, and many people came from outside the home to hear him.

mixed them up.   What so-called Grundtvigians have done concerns me not at all, for they are unknown to me.   I have never been good at starting parties and I have never tried it, for history has taught me that parties share the fate of the lettuce of Epictetus; he who will not pay the price must go without.   If people would take the time, as I have done, to look more closely, they would soon discover that the so-called Grundtvigians differ.   Some might praise my sermon or my song but criticize my bent toward mythology, history, and my extreme Danishness.   They might blame my blindness toward the excellence of revival meetings or mission promotion.   Others would do the opposite.   Even though I might have two halves of a party I would never have a whole one.   Even when I am lauded for both my Danishness and Christianity, the end result always includes the qualification that the Danishness must be christened to be worthy of mention.   This is far from my intent, for I take pains to keep Danishness and Christianity apart.   They are not incompatible, but they are highly different.   The one is valid only in a small corner of the North, the other is universal; the one is temporally determined, the other is valid for time and eternity.

I cannot deny, however, that in my youth I often mentioned Danishness and Christianity in one breath.   The relation was so vague that many believed that I mixed them up.   I am therefore best qualified to illumine a relationship that has been vague in my thoughts and still is vague all over Christendom, namely, the right relationship of folk-life and Christianity.

In regard to the original situation, we all know that Christianity was related to folk-life as a heavenly guest in an earthly home.   This was true even in the land of the Jews where Christianity originated and in heathen countries to which it was transplanted.   The guest came to serve and not to be served, and even though we have erased most of the traces of this in the priestly rule (the hierarchy), it is still true that the original relationship is the only right and natural one. . . .

It is possible that I was wrong in my youth and that I am criticized unjustly in my old age.   As the matter is of utmost concern for folk-life as well as for Christianity,   I must make every effort to clarify for my countrymen and for Danish Christians in particular that the pristine relation was the only right one and that we must make every effort to restore what was disturbed.

When we, first of all, remember how Christianity came to Denmark, we know that it did not come as a violent conqueror who threatens the people with arms and suppression. It came through a meek and defenseless monk, who asked the king of Denmark for permission to proclaim the good news of a savior, born in Bethlehem, and to christen those who were persuaded to believe in Jesus Christ. We know that the king of Denmark gave him this permission, not because he himself was a Christian or had any intention of becoming one but because he found that the evangelist, Ansgar, was a sincere, honest, and loyal man. He drew a conclusion from the servant to the master, from the evangelist to the evangel.

The influence of Christianity in Denmark was thus originally based on the effect of the Word itself in the Danish people. If it had been the intention to sneak into the country, to gather a group of followers, and then to suppress the king as well as the people, this would have been a paltry betrayal. . . .

If this had really been the spirit of Christianity, it would not have been a good spirit. Like the Roman spirit it would have been inimical toward the spirit of all peoples, therefore also inimical toward the spirit of humanity in all its forms, and especially toward the spirit of truth, which is God's own spirit. . . .

The enemies of Christianity themselves admit that violence or deceit are alien to Christianity, even when they persecuted the Christians. If the opposite is true, if the spirit of Christianity is love and truth, then it could never erase and suppress the folk-life. It would do itself a disservice, as the papists have proved. . . .

Only when we realize that a Christian simulation benefits neither the people nor Christianity but that it is detrimental to both can we attempt to place Christianity and the people in a free relationship. This was the original situation in our country and it should prevail wherever Christianity arrives.

The easiest way to this insight is to take a good look at Christianity and realize that it is not, as the papists believed, a new law of God which was to control the world as the law of Moses controlled the Israelites. It is a heavenly gospel, a matchless offer which grants peace to all who accept it, and only to them. . . .

Shortcuts are sly, the adage tells us. Even those who believe that Christianity is the good news and that it profits only those who accept it voluntarily, so that all compulsion is undesirable, even those can maintain that Christianity is accompanied by a law of God which is to check the infidels who do not accept it.

We can also prove, however, that the apology of the Protestants who seek to garnish the spiritual servitude which they practiced as well as condemned is a vain excuse. It was faith in Jesus Christ and his gospel which they would force upon people. They forced a confession of faith from those who had no faith. We cannot rightly loathe a "ruling church" until we acknowledge that law or gospel, claiming divine revelation, can only be true and efficacious when they relate to men in freedom. Every other faith-relationship is false and obnoxious before God and intolerable for a true person. . . . Anyone who claims a divine revelation and uses tyranny and slavery has proved his own sham. No matter what earthly benefit can be derived from his lies and false claims of salvation, it profits not a soul to gain the whole world when one is lost in the abyss of falsehood and deceit.

Not all will acknowledge this proof, for there are those who emulate Pilate in their concern for the truth. The main concern, however, is that all Christians, and particularly Danish Christians, may gain the insight that spiritual servitude in matters of salvation is always as un-Christian and ungodly as it is inhuman. Only when Christians everywhere join up with nature-people will Christianity and folk-life everywhere, and soonest in Denmark, be restored to their original, free, only right, and natural relationship.

It has often been said, and only a fool will deny it, that folk-life has awakened everywhere in Christendom and that it strives everywhere, with more or less insight and power, to exert its influence against alien values which dominate or seek to dominate it for the moment. Christianity appears to be losing its influence in the peoples, but when we clearly see that Christianity rather than seeking it abhors all spiritual servitude, and rather than suppressing it promotes the folk-life, then every people would be insane to reject

an ally against foreign dominance. . . . As far as Denmark is concerned, I am certain that Christianity will gain respect and influence
when it advances the cause of spiritual freedom in the service of
folk-life. This will take place not only because it gains merit with
the suppressed, tortured, and almost inanimate folk-life, but because true Christianity must presuppose spiritual freedom and folk-
life, or if they are absent, create them.

The sixteenth-century Reformers had a vague notion of this when
they helped the people to throw off the yoke imposed upon them by
the pope and his priests in the name of Christianity and under the
false pretext of being God's regent. They introduced the language
of the people into the church as the condition for the living influence
of true Christianity. Therefore, they are praised as heroic figures
or demigods even by those who do not favor the Christianity of the
Reformers. The reformers of the nineteenth century need only to
follow the example of their predecessors in order to broaden and
deepen the influence of Christianity. They will be highly favored
by the peoples, whether these wish to be Christians or not. This
matter must be left to the individuals, but they can decide only
when human nature and Christianity meet in free interaction.

I well know that many orthodox members of the state church
regard spiritual freedom as inimical, and that many sanctified people
regard human nature as something Christianity must combat. This
happens, however, because they do not know a living Christianity
nor the spirit which vitalizes. They have an unspiritual and inanimate concept of both. Every person should know that believing has
more to do with freedom than thinking does. The person who does
not naturally believe in God and does not desire eternal life will not
be aware of the gospel of the Son of God with the Word of eternal
life. Wherever Christianity is to be beneficial it must either presuppose spiritual freedom and folk-life or it must, as mentioned
above, create them.

There are surely those who concede that spiritual freedom and
humanity are presuppositions for Christianity but who deny the
same for folk-life. This happens because they think of humanity as
a life in heaven or in the sky, never on earth. On earth you never
find humanity without folk-life, whether folk-life encompasses hu-

manity or, as in the case of Jesus Christ, humanity encompasses folk-life.

When we, first of all, consider the Hebraic or Israelite folk-life, which is more clearly delineated than our own, inasmuch as all our preachers have preached it and our best children's books have depicted it, we see clearly that everything in the land of the Jews was arranged to maintain and strengthen folk-life. When it languished, it was marvelously awakened by John the Baptist before Christ came. He turned the hearts of children to their parents and the hearts of parents to the children in order that he might pave the way for the Lord and present him with a well-prepared people.

When we then turn to Danish folk-life, which seems very vague because no one has promoted it for centuries but which we all know about in our own nature, we realize that the cause of this lies in the absence of a living folk-life. All zealous ministers and all alert intellectuals lament the prevailing indifference toward spiritual matters, the blindness in regard to the spiritual world, and the deafness which no trumpets can penetrate. We are experiencing a "folk-death" to the extent that the Danishness which is still alive resembles the inconsolable widow at the gates of Nain, escorting her only son to the grave.

To speak to the Danish people about the life in Christ, which is the only living Christianity, is useless under these circumstances. When we yet do it, we sense it is as if our master had spoken to the dead young man on the bier about the way to eternal life which he, of course, did not do. If we therefore wish to accomplish anything in the name of our Lord, we must first of all, as he did, have compassion with the sorrowing widow. To her he said: Weep not!, and to the lad he said: Arise! When temporal life is nonexistent, or when it is a crushing burden in grief, words about eternal life will be useless, if not scorned.

Even when we do not understand why this is, it will continue to persist. The death of Danish folk-life is the spiritual death of the people. It must be remedied by the reawakening of folk-life before we can effectively speak to the people about living Christianity. This is what I have claimed for many years, and in no other manner have I confused Danishness and Christianity. I shall not take responsibility in regard to this for the days of my youth. At that time I dreamt that one must first become a living Christian and then a Dane. Even then my nature prevailed, and I used several of my ardent years in the ministry to translate the ancient chronicles and Beowulf. They could not awaken the folk-life, although they tried. Far less could they make the people Christian.

The reason that a people must become aware of itself before any other spirit than its own can speak to it is the same reason that a person must become self-conscious before it does any good to speak to him about his human needs, about the peril he is in or the means of rescue. We all know that it is the Word which raises humanity above animals. It is the Word by which the world of the spirit is opened and the present life becomes a transition from the open-ended past to the endless future, so that we exist in an eternity we cannot comprehend but which is vital and necessary. Just as the invisible world becomes alive and strong only on the mother tongue, our living relation to our past and our future depends on our sense of continuity with our ancestors and our descendants. If the word of God is to find a well-prepared people, then, in Denmark as in Israel, it is necessary for a word of the people (a folk word) in the mother tongue to turn the hearts of the children to the parents and the hearts of the parents to the children. Then the people can feel that death in any shape is the great enemy and that He is the only savior who can and will give us eternal life.

That this sounds suspicious to many a vicar and even many a bishop, I can well understand. Even I would regard it with suspicion if someone should claim competence to awaken the dead. Even the most cataracted vicar should be able to see, however, that I do not mix up Danishness and Christianity. I separate them more than anyone else who has written up to now. When I desire the school of the people to be Danish, I do not believe that Danishness will make us all-knowing or will gain us salvation. I do so because we must be Danish just as all people must become alive before it is of any use to speak to them about temporal or eternal life. I do not envy those who prefer to speak to the dead, but I repeat that I would rather speak to living robbers than to dead saints. The former might be converted but the latter can do nothing.

About Folk-Life
and Dr. Rudelbach
January 30, 1848

It is not correct, as the *Berlingske* daily idly infers, that Dr. Rudelbach has accused me of "egoistical folkliness," according to which Christianity should be adjusted or maladjusted. Nevertheless, Dr. Rudelbach has expressed dissatisfaction with the piece I recently wrote in *Kirketidende* about "Christianity and Folk-Life." With all his learning he seeks to disprove my simple postulate that folk-life is a necessary prerequisite for living Christianity.

Without commenting on the concepts about nationality, as false and un-Christian as they are egoistical, which the doctor conjures out of German and French books in order to combat them, I will merely sweep my own doorstep and try to clarify more distinctly what I mean by that folk-life, which I claim has always been and always will be a necessary prerequisite for a living Christianity here on earth. I thought I had said this so succinctly that it would be understood, if not by all learned men then certainly by a learned man who has known me as long as Dr. Rudelbach has and who knows as much history as he does. He declares, however, that he still does not see how that which I call folk-life is obviously different from the un-Christian and anti-Christian nationalism which is proclaimed in Germany and France. I will therefore, for his sake and for the sake of all my countrymen, try to make myself clear.

I assume that all my attentive listeners and readers, including, therefore, Dr. Rudelbach, know that when I speak of the folk-life that is a prerequisite for Christianity I do not imply that it is a substitute for Christianity or that it qualifies a people for Christianity. I must, however, expressly call attention to this, inasmuch as the doctor has confused all three parts in his little book *Chris-*

tianity and Nationality, thereby diligently proving what I have never questioned, that even Israel did not have a nationality which could substitute for Christianity or qualify the people for it.

My simple and historic ideas about this matter are that God unquestionably had good reasons for not sending his Son, born of a woman, in the days of Abraham's descendants to the people of Israel which he led through its natural stages before he sent them his Son in the fullness of time. The folk-life of this people of Israel is thus the necessary prerequisite for the advent of Christ. John the Baptist revitalized the memories, the hope, and the imagery of the people, and without this awakening to folk-consciousness Christianity would not have been known, understood, or believed in Israel.

I do not believe that Dr. Rudelbach and I disagree about this, inasmuch as there was no mention of merit on the part of the people. I spoke only about the natural conditions for the living arrival of Christianity and its fruitful action in the world. The condition for the real humanity of God's Son was that he was born into the world of a woman.

Dr. Rudelbach must therefore believe that Christianity could come to us in a living way and that it could come alive in us without the same essential conditions with which it came alive for and in the individuals of Israel who had it in their hearts to believe the Son. He must believe that this could happen without a revitalization of the memories, the hope, and the imagery of the people. Because this opinion has prevailed among men of learning for hundreds of years, it is no surprise to meet it in Dr. Rudelbach. I had hoped and expected, however, that he would not have denounced my ideas so quickly. He must know that I have not concocted them out of thin air but that they originate in a folk-historic consideration in the light of Christianity—a consideration which must be tried and tested before it is discarded along with the pantheistic and anti-Christian notions of others.

For it is an unshakable fact, evident to all who know the Scriptures, that we are far from living in the world in the same manner that Christ was. We are far from any valid comparison with the apostolic congregation in Jerusalem. Yet a thorough appropriation and revelation of the life of Christ in his faithful believers is obviously the living Christianity which the apostles describe and which they demand of all believers. If we do not have this, the fault is not God's; it must lie with us. To discover why we have not seen the likeness of the apostolic congregation or a living Christianity in a true Christian sense for seventeen hundred years is undeniably a task for Christian scholars. They must not take to this lightly, for the cause must be found before the fault can be remedied.

It is easily seen and said that it is because of our sins that Christianity is not revealed as a divine and living power to us. But it was expressly for the sake of our sins that Christ and Christianity came into the world with the joyful message that they can and will remove our sins, can and will awaken the spiritually dead and bring sinners salvation. We have therefore given no reason for Christianity's poor performance and sad figure among us when we say that our sins are the cause. The sixteenth-century Reformers, particularly Martin Luther, admitted and stressed this constantly. They did not have the delusion that we stopped sinning when we turned our backs to the pope in Rome, eliminated the Mass, ridiculed picture worship, prayed and sang in the vernacular, and read the Bible. The Reformers—Martin Luther in particular—insisted only that these were the necessary conditions for the life of Christianity among us. I am far from contradicting or weakening these postulates of the Reformers and of Martin Luther in particular. When the postulates are carried even further, however, by saying that the sixteenth-century Reformation met all the conditions under which Christianity can develop full apostolic activity, then we are not only going beyond what Martin Luther said, we have already been refuted by three hundred years of church history. For history tells us that even though there were more spiritual and Christian signs of life in Protestant Christendom than in the papal, an apostolic congregation was far from realization. Such a congregation would have been evident if the Word of God was in full strength and all the conditions for life were present.

As I hearken to Holy Writ and especially to its account of Christ, the apostles, and the apostolic congregation, it is my postulate that there are yet many conditions which must be met before that fullness of time will arrive in heathendom which came to Israel with the incarnation of our Lord. To those basic conditions belong not only civic freedom of religion but a living consideration of the Word of God and the nature of man. The consideration of both must come alive before any interaction can take place. There was a necessary but faint start toward this when the sixteenth-century Reformers decisively separated the sacraments instituted by the Lord, baptism and Communion, from all other so-called churchly customs, and when they introduced the vernacular in the church.

Both of these acts had to take place before a spiritual and Christian advance could come. Only then was it apparent where the living Word of God and the lively nature of man were to be found. We cannot say that the sixteenth-century Reformers found them there, for even Martin Luther, who had a strong feeling that they were there, saw only glimpses and did not trust his own eyes in this regard. When there was continuous talk about "the Word and the sacraments," as if a Christian sacrament existed without the Word, Martin Luther refuted this backward talk by his testimony that without the Word of God the water remained water and there was no baptism. Without the Word "This is my body!" and "Given for you!" the Supper was not a divine means of grace. Yet Luther used the backward expression "the Word and the sacraments," and he was confused about the difference between God's living Word, the Holy Scriptures, and the preaching of the scribes. This difference must be clarified before we can find the living Word of God which alone can take our sins away and grant us eternal life.

On the other hand, the sixteenth-century Reformers considered the use of the vernacular in the church to be essential. They believed it to be necessary, however, only because it was impossible to teach Latin to all people. For that reason they had to come down to using an everyday language or continuing without the understanding of the people. This view of the language is so superficial that even though Dr. Rudelbach seems to wish it was the right one, he still will not acknowledge it. But I dare insist that the proclaimers of Christianity must master the language of the people before they can be understood by a people. If the people really are to see, hear, and find what the spirit of the Lord, as a foreign guest, has to give, and what the essentials are, they must have a living participation through their natural imagery, for this is where the living proclamation of Christianity of necessity must begin. As it is with the mother tongue, so it is with the life of peoples. Just as human language has a living presence only in the mother tongue, so can the human race exist only in a folk-life. Human beings must be confronted where they really exist if they are to be persuaded to believe in Jesus Christ.

It is of no use to call upon the Scriptures which say that all men are sinners and that there is no difference in this regard, for in Christianity there is neither Jew nor Greek, Scythian nor barbarian. The question before us has nothing to do with merit, nor with what we find in Christ or Christianity. It has to do with what is really in the world and how the world can become Christian in spirit and in truth. I am never in doubt that God is the same toward all peoples, whatever their grouping, nor that God's Son could have revealed himself as a human being or as an angel before King Dan as he did for Abraham. But if I have to believe the Scriptures then I have to believe that the incarnation of God's Son required that he was conceived and born of a woman. He could find his mother only in a prophetic people chosen by God and led to this. As it was with God's Son's revelation for Israel, I conclude that it is with his revelation for all of us. It is even more evident where his revelation is a spiritual one than it was in the land of the Jews where he was visibly present. In order to know, understand, and appropriate him in a living way we must be guided, enlivened, and enlightened as a people. If this does not happen, we have no living concepts about the relationship between God and man or between time and eternity, life or death in a spiritual sense, between the people of God and the peoples of the world. All these are matters about which we must have living notions if we are, in a vital manner, to be addressed by the gospel of God. Otherwise we shall misunderstand, in a physical manner, all talk about a divine savior, about reconciliation, justification by faith, entrance into the kingdom, membership in the people of God, and the transition to eternal life.

Basic Christian Teachings[14]
The Christianity of the New Testament

It is commonly known that the term "New Testament" in daily speech means nothing more or less than the sacred scripture of Christians, in contrast to that sacred scripture which in its essence is Jewish and which was called "Old Testament" by the Christians. But inasmuch as "testament" is a foreign term which even in the legal language derived from Roman law means the last will of a deceased, few people know what the book title of our Christian sacred scripture really means. This would not be important if the same term was not used for something other than the book. The term "New Testament" shares the fate, however, of the term "church," and we have, out of carelessness, given the same name to two basically different items. This always causes some confusion, and it can lead to unbounded confusion when unwise or crafty persons take charge.

When we used a foreign word to designate both the Christian congregation and our Sunday-houses with their caretakers, calling both of them *"Kirke"* [church], even the most honest and sensible mention of these widely different concerns became ambiguous. When crafty priests and popes put themselves in the Lord's place and elevated outward concerns over the inward, they had a great opportunity in the ambiguity of speech as well as thought.

The same thing happened when all of Christendom on the one hand and the Sunday-Book with the scribes on the other were given the same name, "the New Testament." By this common term even the most honest and informed speech about totally different things

14. Between 1855 and 1861 Grundtvig wrote a series of essays which he entitled *Christian Childhood Teachings*. In this volume they are called "Basic Christian Teachings."

49

was made ambiguous.   When vain and ambitious teachers and
scribes usurped the place of the spirit, and when book-reading replaced the faith, this ambiguity of speech and interpretation gave
them their desired opportunity.

The fact is, of course, that the Greek word *"diatheke,"* which
becomes *"testamentum"* in Latin, means both a covenant and what we
call a testament.   In Greek all of Christendom could be called *"kaine
diatheke,"* the new covenant; in Latin, however, *"novum testamentum"*
or our own word, "the New Testament," which is half-Latin and
half-Danish, does not cover this.   Nevertheless, we have applied the
term "the New Testament" both to our version of the Bible and to
the Lord's speech to us in the Holy Communion, to Christendom as
a whole, while we, at the same time, use it for the writings of the
apostles.   The uninformed and crafty therefore can easily confuse the
two by saying: "the New Testament," this and this alone is Christianity!   But they mean the book, so that the cup of the New
Testament becomes the cup of the written letter, and the office-
holders of the New Testament become the office-holders of the
written letter, even though the apostle plainly writes that he does
not consider them servants of the letter but, contrariwise, of the
spirit.

It makes no difference, of course, whether we call the apostolic
writings "the New Testament" or "the new book" or "the book of
the new covenant," but this matter has been the cause of great
confusion when we gave the book the same name as the spirit and
life of Christianity.   By a well-concealed play on words the letter
could be put in the place of the spirit, and a written testament could
be put in place of a living covenant.   If this dreadful confusion is to
be cleared up, we must begin by speaking plainly: The new covenant between the Lord and us is the covenant of baptism, which is
established for all those who wish to be baptized in the name of the
Father and the Son and the Holy Spirit, as the Lord instituted it.
Thereby, they who are baptized are inseparably related to the triune
God by the confession of faith in their baptismal covenant, without
reference to that book which we call the New Testament.

There is not the slightest reason for someone to say that this
statement is derogatory toward the apostolic scriptures.   It is not
only a fact that the new covenant was established and has been

established at baptism down through the ages without the slightest reference to the apostolic scriptures.   It is also obvious that when the Lord and his apostles instituted baptism, and thereby the new covenant, they could not have considered a scripture which did not exist.   We can no more do this than could they without deviating independently from the Lord and his apostles, stunting his covenant and its institution.   Finally, the apostolic scriptures never pretend to be "the new covenant" or to be the foundation for Christianity.

On the contrary, they refer constantly to an oral word of God, a covenant of the heart and a living foundation.

When it is claimed, however, that my contention that the covenant of baptism, the foundational expression of Christianity as far as its validity goes, is independent of the apostolic scriptures should mean that the apostolic scriptures have nothing to do with the covenant of baptism, either in regard to affirmation, information, or interpretation, then the contention of another is substituted for mine.   I have always diligently demonstrated that the fact that the scriptures do presuppose the covenant of baptism and the confession of faith verifies the genuine apostolic character of the scriptures.   On the other hand, the apostolic scriptures contribute inexpressibly much to the information about the covenant of baptism and its true Christian explanation, and we find it to be indispensable.

When it is finally said, as it has been done recently, that there is no occasion for dispute, but rather all possible cause for agreement between those who acknowledge that both the covenant of baptism and the apostolic scriptures belong to the basics of Christianity, which are not to be altered but always better to be understood, then this is precisely my conviction and contention from the start.   This has not been admitted, and the agreement shall not prevent me but rather press me to give all the information I am able to give about the right relationship between the covenant of baptism and the apostolic scriptures.   This relationship has been so distorted that the book was not only put in the place of the covenant but was made the presupposition for the covenant.   The book is the work of the apostles and the property of the congregation, but it was made into a letter of call for the apostles and a book of law for the congregation.

[Grundtvig declares that he is willing to accept as Christians all who accept the covenant of baptism and use it, but that he will also combat any misunderstanding of the significance of the baptismal covenant. The *apologia*, unfortunately, has been turned over to the secular authorities, who have used the law to maintain the purity of the gospel. The result has been an outward restrictiveness and an inward indifference toward true understanding of the Christian faith and its relationships.]

Only now, when papists, Baptists, atheists, and Mormons have been given religious freedom and thereby gained boldness and room for action, and when an excellent hairsplitter,[15] presupposing the possible truth of Christianity even in the most unlikely forms, raises the banner for what he calls the Christianity "of the New Testament," by which he exclusively understands the apostolic writings and the Christianity of the letter, only now is there restlessness in the camp. All those who have no Christian faith feel the necessity to defend it against those who boldly insist that we have none or can have none. They who up to now were quick to interchange or confuse the book, "The New Testament," with the new covenant between the Lord and us concerning a clear conscience and a blessed eternity are now compelled to admit that their thinking was askew or even backward and that it cannot be defended.

For the hairsplitter tells them: You and I agree that the Christianity of the New Testament is the only right one. Now you insist that the Christianity you preach on Sundays, teach your confirmands, use to comfort your church-goers and confessors, describe in your books, enforce by civil law and are salaried to uphold, use as a means of comfortable living and the accumulation of titles and decorations, that this is and has to be the Christianity of the New Testament. But either you know nothing about the New Testament, and then you are blind guides, or else you must know that this is, deucedly, not the Christianity of the New Testament but even the very opposite, and then you are, as far as Christianity is concerned, consummate rascals. Now, the hairsplitter pretends that he did not know the Christian covenant of baptism or the means of salvation, baptism and Communion, or he acts as if they were minor details that were not to be considered in the discussion of New Testament Christianity. In order to make out that all of

15. Søren Kierkegaard.

Christendom is contrary to the Christianity of the New Testament he uses all possible tricks and deceits, as if true Christianity could impossibly be proclaimed or propagated in a so-called state church, because this is in its totality an un-Christian hodgepodge. He carries on as if anything he can refute by prooftexting is thereby eternally made un-Christian. The result invariably is that he puts the cart before the horse, and he does this consistently. Every day it becomes more obvious that if we do not wish to concede that the hairsplitter was right we must drop the backward procedure. We must deny that the book, "The New Testament," is the real source, foundation, and Rule of Faith, for this is the criterion of the hairsplitter as a judge of Christianity and a torturer of ministers. He must either refute himself or else stand as an apparent enemy and despiser of Christianity. . . .

[The next paragraph repeats the argument that Christianity has its origin in a living word rather than in written Scripture. This is important, not only for an evaluation of Christianity but also for a personal acceptance and relationship.]

I have therefore constantly emphasized that the new life, which is participation in God's only-begotten Son, the righteous, true, sacred, and eternally blessed human life of our Lord Jesus Christ, can only be communicated to us by a spoken word of God to us. It is therefore fantasy when someone imagines that this new Christian life can be appropriated out of the clear sky, or as the wind blows, or through the stroke of a pen in a book, or by a word of God that is not spoken to us, or by a priestly word, or a papal word, or a scholarly word to us, no matter how true it is or how well it can be documented. When our Lord Jesus Christ is to save us from death and grant us eternal life, he must have left on earth a spoken word of God for us, a word of his own institution, which is "Spirit and Life," which can save us, and which shows us that salvation is his work, not the work of a pope or ourselves. The Spirit and Life we get from the word of his mouth is clearly his own spirit and life, not ours or that of anyone else.

This is my understanding of the so-called words of institution at baptism and Communion which give life.

[Two additional pages of argument are not included.]

Basic Christian Teachings
The Christian Signs of Life

Throughout the entire history of Christianity all serious-minded people who have been attracted to its promise of eternal salvation have been aware that salvation could not have been an eternal concern without an evident influence on our temporal life. Those who deny this and expect from Christianity only a "blessed death" reveal that they are spiritually defunct and that they expose Christianity to the well-deserved scorn of the unbelieving world. If the gospel of Christ were only a so-called word of eternal life which deadened the temporal life even more than previously, no truth-loving person could believe it. Whatever is spiritually dead and powerless or even without spirit in our temporal existence could not possibly be spiritually alive and powerful in eternity. Our Lord Jesus Christ has given testimony that we must be reborn spiritually in the course of time in order to participate in eternal life, and he witnesses that this is a truth about the earthly existence which must be accepted before we can believe the truth about the heavenly experience.

Although the concept of Christianity held by the papists was as dead and powerless as possible without apparent contradiction, even they gave serious emphasis to a so-called Christian life, namely, the monastic life. This was alleged to be the possession of the whole church, and every member could take part in it by believing it and by contributing, each according to his ability, to the maintenance, welfare, and elevation of this so-called godly and Christian monastic life. That this monastic life, even with the halo of saints, was a spiritual and Christian pretense which revealed the spiritual death which it made efforts to hide has been so clearly exposed by church history that it needs no further documentation, at least not among the disciples of Martin Luther.

Turning now to the disciples of Martin Luther, the so-called Lutherans, it cannot be denied that they spoke and wrote themselves out on a limb when they claimed that the basically ungodly and unimprovable temporal life of man must be canceled out in the matters of salvation. They emphasized "a blessed death," quoting the wise preacher who said that the day of death is better than the day of birth. [Eccles. 7:1] Like their Calvinistic counterparts the Lutheran dogmatics were based on the dead letter and on the Scripture principle, and inasmuch as the academic life of the scholars was even less godly than that of the monks, the papists had a good argument when they accused us of having an even more lifeless concept of Christianity than they. But even then the Lutherans have chosen the better part and placed themselves on the side of life, for they left the spiritually dead pseudo-life to the papists and put their trust in the spirit which could make them alive in Christianity despite their apparent death.

Even while the Lutherans condemned the natural life of man and despite their praise of "the blessed death" and "the blessed corpses," they still make serious demands for a living faith as a requirement for true Christianity. This faith was to demonstrate its spiritual power and its reality in a living confession, proclamation, and song of praise in the mother tongue. We now make bold to declare that we thereby have given name to the Christian signs of life, which must never be entirely absent in true Christianity and which never can be found together except where the spirit of the Lord, which creates life, is the divine spokesman, comforter, and guide to the truth for the congregation.

What caused the everyday catalepsy among even the true Lutherans and stunted the growth of Christian life was the confused and contradictory ideas about evangelical freedom with state church servitude, rebirth in baptism with Scripture-living, and finally the Christian renewal of life without the benefit of a previous human life that could be renewed. When we now, by the grace of God, see the light of the Lord, the confession will be more firm and full, the proclamation far more simple and forceful, and the song of praise far more clear and delightful. All of our temporal human life will thereby gain a spiritual and hearty renewal, whose Christianity perhaps cannot be strictly documented but whose nature is sure. For this noble and hearty form of living will only be found where the Christian confession, proclamation, and song of praise are openly present. We have recently seen that this insight is a rarity among us, for when Søren Kierkegaard a few moments ago sought to frighten us out of our wits by his black-chalk drawing of the "mendicant monk" as the only true disciple of Christ, who literally carried his cross and followed him, he was confronted by a deep ignorance about the Christian life. In corners,[16] however, he graciously met the morning light which gives glow to life and which urged him on by the dark cloud to vigorous advances on his heroic career.

In this situation[17] it became clearly evident that all discussion and polemics about the Christian life is futile when we do not presuppose and maintain that the Christian congregation, created by the baptism of the Lord's own institution, has its peculiar source of life in this baptism and in it alone. The congregation's confession of faith at baptism is therefore the one and only Christian confession, and as a living expression of the Christian faith it is the first and last sign of

16. By "corners" Grundtvig undoubtedly means the out-of-the-way places where Kierkegaard met Grundtvig's views about faith and worship, such as worship services and Grundtvig's writings, which would be "corners" to Kierkegaard.

17. It is at this point that Grundtvig meets Søren Kierkegaard's concept of Christian living head on. In the polemics, usually called "Attack Upon Christendom," which occupied Kierkegaard in the months before his death in 1855, he had maintained that the signs of Christian living are to be found in personal discipleship, guided by the teachings of Jesus, the inevitable consequences of which would be the cross of suffering. The demands of this discipleship are so great that no one can claim to be a true follower and that no one, therefore, is or ever has been a true Christian. Out of consideration for Kierkegaard Grundtvig waited some time after Kierkegaard's death before he took up the subject. Now he characterizes Kierkegaard's description of the Christian life in the stark terms of "a black-chalk drawing of a mendicant monk." In contrast to Kierkegaard's strong demand for personal and ethical discipleship, Grundtvig makes the claim that the only signs of Christian life are found in the fellowship of worship with its proclamation of the gospel, its confession of faith, and its songs of praise. The Christian life is not a separate, disciplined life; it is a true human life which is not a life different from the created life of mankind. The created life has been reborn and renewed through its participation with God in the worship, particularly in the sacraments, but the new life is nonetheless a human life. The Christian life is a human life, the fruits of which will make its renewal manifest. Out of personal acquaintance Grundtvig knew that Kierkegaard was familiar with the worship renewal that was taking place in Danish church life, and he claimed that Kierkegaard had "graciously met the morning light" of the gospel in the "corners." There is a contrast here between the imposing cathedral in which Bishop Mynster preached, and which Kierkegaard could see from his windows, and the modest sanctuary around the corner from Kierkegaard's home, where Grundtvig preached and where there was a strong and growing renewal of congregational fellowship.

Christian life. With this basic insight into the Christian life as a faith-life, and with this illumination of the confession of faith of the congregation as the true sign of life, it is readily seen that the Christian life can and must be revealed ever more strongly and more clearly in a living proclamation and song of praise corresponding to the confession. The entire history of the Christian church must demonstrate whether the new Christian life is more or less human than the old human life, which was lived before Christ, or that human life which is alive today without baptismal faith in Christ and without the rebirth to Christ's human life in the baptism of his own institution.

It could be asserted boldly that this basic teaching (childhood teaching) is contrary to Scripture, for the polemics about the right interpretation of departed writers is endless. Book knowledge and Scripture knowledge differ so vastly that even if all Christians were avid readers only a few of them could have real grounds for a conviction about the biblical character of Christianity or the Christianity of the Bible. We Christian scribes, however, will correctly and at all times defend the claim that our Sacred Scripture does not contradict our basic Christian teaching about "faith and baptism." On the contrary, there is complete agreement. The confession of faith is even given a wondrous testimony by a word of the Lord: "Every one who acknowledges me before men, the Son of man also will acknowledge before the angels of God" [Luke 12:8].

In an outward manner we must therefore necessarily first and last emphasize the confession of faith, even as we inwardly emphasize faith. In the new life the confession corresponds to breathing in the old. Be it far from our purpose, however, to exclude the proclamation or the song of praise as signs of life. As little can they be excluded, where the life born of faith is to thrive, as the life born of faith can gain and grow to maturity without hope and love. These are in relation to the living proclamation and song of praise as faith is to confession. Where confession is the only sign of life, the faith-life will be weak and sickly and it will be tempted to death in every trial. This throws light on the fact that the Christian faith was originally given birth by the proclamation of him who came from above and plainly spoke "the Word of God." As the apostle states it, faith is propagated only by the living proclamation of the word of faith. He asks: "How are men to call upon him in whom they have not believed?" But he also asks: "How are they to hear without a preacher?" [Rom. 10:14].

The Christian confession of faith can be found and has been found alive in a situation where the proclamation of faith largely is dead in the church, but the confession is then moribund and it will take the faith with it into the grave. Or it might be revived to re-create the living proclamation even as unmistakably happened through Martin Luther.

What happened with us in the beginning of our own century had evidently happened all over Christendom in the beginning of the sixteenth century. At that time the living proclamation of the Word of faith seemed to be almost dead or so obviously close to death that it had to be wondrously reborn in order to propagate the faith from generation to generation. It was obviously thus reborn through Martin Luther who proclaimed the "Word of Faith" with spirit and life in the mother tongue. Luther thereby enlivened the proclamation not only among the kinfolk in England and the Nordic countries; he influenced even the Romance peoples, most evidently among the Calvinists but apparently everywhere.

This great wonder did not demonstrate "universal priesthood" as much as the Calvinists believed, for Martin Luther was himself ordained. The wonder was demonstrated, however, by the renewal of the proclamation that the priests of Christendom have no charter or monopoly on the proclamation of the gospel. Nor have they spiritual domination over the institutions of the Lord.

Martin Luther did not credit his ordination with merit in his calling or in his competence to proclaim the gospel. On the contrary, he took away all the claim of the ordination as a sacrament for the faithful. It was evidently not his ordination that enabled the rebirth of a living proclamation of the gospel through him. This rebirth is a much greater wonder of God than the ordinary continuation of the proclamation could be.

Ordination can be, even in the face of Luther's denial, what I believe it to be, a spiritual means of grace for the Christian scholar who has faith. It can never, however, in spite of Lutheran evidence, give color to any papacy or hierarchy. We must rightly understand the apostle when he speaks about the proclamation of the word and asks: "How can men preach unless they are sent?" [Rom. 10:15]. On the one hand we may think about the immediate and visible sending, which ordination with the laying on of hands really is. On the other hand, the apostle Paul cannot exclusively have considered sending to be this. He himself was an exception and he expresses this quite often. In a manner known only to him he was sent by the ascended Lord to proclaim the gospel. Martin Luther was, of course, greatly influenced by Paul, and it is understandable that he clung to the Pauline commissioning in the face of the pope and his miscreant priests. But we cannot quite accept this one-sidedness by which the exception is made the rule. On behalf of the apostle Paul we must even argue with Martin Luther that the apostle himself was dedicated as a traveling missionary by the laying on of hands, but that Paul ascribes to the laying on of hands by the elders a priestly gift of the spirit. Finally, Paul admits that there is a special commissioning to baptize which he did not have. Even with all this, the fact remains that the ascended Lord has reserved the right, even without human mediation, to commission preachers by his spirit, and these may baptize whom they please. No priesthood can therefore, no matter how genuinely apostolic it is, have a Christian basis for claiming a monopoly on preaching or on baptism. Priests may not claim dominion over the Christian light or over the Christian life. Under certain circumstances the reaction to alleged dominion may breed what we call "revivals" or "godly assemblies," whose genuine Christianity nevertheless is not to be opposed by the priesthood as irresponsible lay efforts. They are to be judged in the same manner that priesthood is judged, by their relation to the Christian confession, proclamation, and song of praise, and in an insoluble relation to baptism, which opens the Christian founts of life, and with Holy Communion, which creates and upholds the Christian stream of life in community with the Lord.

Just as the congregation's confession of faith at baptism is the undeviating rule for all Christian confession and is the core of all Christian proclamation of the gospel, so must all Christian life exclusively be derived from the work of the Lord with his spoken word—in baptism and in Communion. Only when the Christian life is thus elevated does the song of praise of the congregation become Christian. It was a sure sign of spiritual death in the papal church that the song of praise of the congregation on the mother tongue had died away, and the congregational song in the mother tongue in the Lutheran church is a clear sign of life and a valid witness to the Christian character of the Lutheran preaching. The song of praise will always correspond to the proclamation, for the song is the congregational answer to the address of the proclamation. The Calvinist preaching in the mother tongue engendered a corresponding song, but this took a Jewish not a Christian shape and thus denied the Christian life of the Calvinistic preaching. The cause for this was the superior attitude toward the fount of life in baptism and the life-stream of the Supper. As long as baptism and the Supper were regarded as shadowy images of either circumcision or the paschal lamb or as images of rebirth and nurture, it was not easy dry-shod to cross the Red Sea and enter into the promised land.

To be sure, the Lutheran preaching and song of praise also had their faults and wants, inasmuch as they did not clearly enough relate the "faith" to the "Word of Faith" in baptism. Therefore, they could not in a clear and living manner derive the Christian life from its fountain and flow, in the Lord's own word and action in baptism and Communion. Nevertheless, the Lutheran proclamation and song of praise still had a vague understanding and a living expression of a real presence of the Word of God and the life-giving power of the Lord's own institutions. Therefore, the Christian life became more vigorous and more evident than had been the case for many centuries. The shortcomings of the Lutheran proclamation and song of praise have, in a way, straightened themselves out, i.e., they have been corrected by the Spirit in the congregational confession and the life in the Lord's institution. Therefore we claim that the faults had their cause only in the lack of light and power, which can hardly be expected in infancy. It is a matter of course that the newborn preaching and song were tender and frail in the days and in the mouth of Martin Luther.

Hereby it is best seen how objectionable and inappropriate any other norm for teaching than the Holy Scriptures and the undeviating altar book and hymnal have been and must be for the Christian growth of the Lutheran preaching and song. Even in the most tolerable form all other norms must be likened to a disciplined, monotonous, and restricted diet, which might be appropriate in old age and which can prevent disease and even delay death, but which stunts childhood development and thwarts all further growth. If, therefore, the two blessed offspring of Luther, the reborn Christian preaching and the song of praise of the people, are to grow to maturity by the power of the Spirit so that their glory will ever exist on earth, as we hope and pray the case may be despite all sulking and deviation by deadbeats, then we must give ample room for proclamation and song of praise as the spirit wills it in the realm of confession. This is the right "evangelical freedom," the freedom to eat the fruits of all the trees in the garden except the tree of death, which is that Scripture knowledge and theology which usurp the place of God by judging his words and deeds, namely, his word to us and his work within us. When we fail to build on and rest within the testimony of the Spirit and the congregation about the Christian faith and confession and about the Lord's institution as actions by his own word, which is his and his alone, and if we instead doubt this foundation for the faith and the church's fount of life and put ourselves in the judge's seat to determine if we have this Word of God and if this is good and true and can bring us salvation, then we stand like Eve by the forbidden tree, counseling with the serpent about which fruits are good and beneficial for good and evil. Then the scripture will apply which says: "But I am afraid that as the serpent deceived Eve by his cunning, your thoughts will be led astray from a sincere and pure devotion to Christ" [2 Cor. 11:3].

Turning now to the problem of the Christian certainty of the individual in his concern for salvation, which recently has been drawn into the dispute about the validity of baptism administered according to the ritual of the altar book, then we will, as in all matters of Christian information, find no complete answers in any book of dogmatics. Even here, however, the great Lutheran basis for Christian enlightenment, the one of the Word and the faith, is useful and firm. The papists are, of course, right in claiming that the individual must build his certainty of salvation on his participation in the faith, hope, and love of the whole church, but it was Martin Luther's bold stroke to refer the individual to the inner testimony of the Holy Spirit as the only assurance of God's grace and eternal life. This venture was made necessary by the contamination of the concept of the church by the hierarchy and their compulsory baptism. For just as God is the God of the living and not of the dead, so is the Holy Spirit the spirit of the living church and not of a dead one. It is a false and pernicious certainty in matters of salvation to rely on a spiritually dead church where the Christian means of grace, baptism and Communion, are distorted or out of function. Such a church is like a priestly insurance company where an annual contribution in an outward way guarantees its members against spiritual fire damage in purgatory and hell. Martin Luther was right when he declared this to be fraud and even murder, as the claim was made to avoid hell or enter heaven. When Luther constantly referred to that external and clear word of God by which we can learn to know and understand the Holy Spirit, then his mistake was only this, as it was in all of his evangelical service, that he confused his biblical preaching with the confession of faith and the words of institution, as if everything was a clear word of God whereby we could know and understand the Holy Spirit. We must separate what we, and not the Lord, have joined together. The confession of faith by the congregation at baptism, according to the institution of the Lord, then becomes the clear standard for the congregation and its spirit. It is then evident that as members of this congregation, which is the Christian and spiritual people of God, we can reach the same certainty in matters of salvation as the congregation has in its consideration of the Christian signs of life, the confession, the proclamation, and the song of praise. These signs of life will become clearer and stronger in relation to the freedom these three enjoy. On the other hand, all external compulsion in spiritual matters will weaken the expressions of life and conceal its signs. No one can be certain of the genuine and firm character of Christian confession if the confession is required by law and nonconfession is liable to civil punishment. So then, the Christian proclamation and song of praise will never be the strong expressions and signs which give assurance of strength and growth unless they have external freedom.   Opponents of freedom for preachers and hymn-writers therefore, consciously or unconsciously, place obstacles in the way of the Spirit who works only in freedom and therefore against the certainty of salvation.   When spiritual freedom is a reality, however, we can boldly answer every faithful Christian who questions the validity of baptism: "Why ask me? Ask the Holy Spirit!   He who is the spirit of faith and baptism will tell you if you are born of water and spirit to enter the kingdom of heaven.   If you are not, he will show you the way."

Basic Christian Teachings
The Christian, the Spiritual, and the Eternal Life

In our day it is so difficult to be understood when one speaks about the real life, as it is lived daily among us and before our very eyes, that everyone who writes about it can surely expect to be grossly misunderstood by most readers. If we are not believed when we write about earthly things, how can we be believed when we write about the heavenly? It is therefore almost miraculous that some people still speak and write about the Christian, the spiritual, and the eternal life. Apparently no one practices it; and from the time of creation until now only one person has carried it through, namely, the only-begotten, the unequaled, "Jesus Christ," who was crucified under Pontius Pilate and is now seated in heaven at the right hand of God, whence he shall come on the final day to judge the living and the dead.

It was therefore no trick for Søren Kierkegaard, as he was applauded by the world, to describe our so-called Christian preaching, Bible-reading, worship, infant baptism, and Communion as an immense tomfoolery and a merry farce. But this became tragicomical, yea, not only greatly tragic but even mockery, when many people came to believe that we so-called ministers, we "black-gowns," were deceiving them. We were telling them that if they would just listen to us with approval, let their infants be baptized, and go to Communion on occasion, then they were participating in a secret and incomprehensible manner, yet in a real sense, in the Christian, the spiritual, and the eternal life, as our Lord Jesus Christ had lived it on earth and promised it eternally to his faithful followers.

This was no trick, and Søren Kierkegaard was careful not to write that he, either by his own insight or out of the New Testament, had gained a light and a power to live a real Christian, spiritual, and eternal life which he could transmit to others. On the contrary, he writes that out of his own experience and out of the New Testament he has learned and can clearly demonstrate that all which pretends to be a Christian, spiritual, and eternal life as it is described in the New Testament, the true and infallible account of the life and teachings of Jesus Christ, is a coarse lie and a monstrous delusion, even an enormous blasphemy. By this he has obviously pledged his own honor and the New Testament to the Danish readers to the contention that no Christian, spiritual, and eternal life exists on earth. It is therefore not only up to us but up to that Jesus Christ, whom we confess, and to that Spirit which guides and comforts us, to show the world that such a life does exist, even though it has long been hidden and is hard to recognize.

It is quite evident that the solution to this unequaled task of living can be given only to a small degree by the pen. It is obvious that we cannot by our pens create such a Christian life, when even the Lord's apostles could not to the slightest degree transplant it or communicate it by their pens, even though we assume that their hand was guided by Christ's spirit. It is also clear as daylight that when we claim that the apostolic writings themselves did not possess or lead a Christian, spiritual, and eternal life we cannot without contradiction ascribe to these writings the ability to transplant or communicate the Christian life which they themselves did not possess or lead. We cannot without blasphemy or ridiculous pride ascribe to our own writings that divine power of living and transfer of life which we deny to the apostolic writings.

The apostolic writings, however, by being a true description of the life of Jesus Christ and of the Christian life as it was found in those who wrote and those who lived it in the Christian congregation, and by being a prophecy of the growth of Christian life in the congregation until it reaches the goal and pattern set by Jesus' own life, can be useful and illuminating for those who believe in Jesus Christ and participate in the Christian life. In the same manner our writings can be useful and illuminating for living Christians, in part when they give a truthful description of the ways and means whereby the present weak, vague, and obscure Christian life has been transmitted to us, and in part when they are a prophecy of how the Christian life will grow in the history of the church until it reaches the fullness, strength, and clarity of the Lord.

To this end I have devoted a lifetime of writing, seeking as well as I might and with great diligence to give the information that it is by the Word of the Lord's own mouth, as it is spoken at baptism and Communion and by nothing else, that his Spirit and his power of living are communicated. His spiritual life disappears where we reject or falsify this Word spoken by the Lord, and the Christian life will be untraceable, where we might maintain this Word unaltered, but only half believe it, and expect spirit, life, and growth by other channels as well.

From the perplexity in the days of Søren Kierkegaard as well as the confusion that existed during the recent polemics about "altar-book baptism," it is obvious that the usefulness of my writings has not been as great as I might desire. I had not expected much else, as long as the Christian life, which cannot emerge or grow through book-writing, has not been more widespread or more clearly developed through "the Word and the Faith" at baptism and Communion than all signs show it to be. I hope, however, that my brief description of "The Christian Signs of Life" may have prepared a growing information about the cause of Christian living which we have missed up to now.

It is a Christian insight, which will shed light on the matter even though it does not completely clarify it, that we must and shall sum up the signs of Christian life in "Confession, Proclamation, and Praise" in the language of the people. I have strongly felt the absence of this when I searched for the Christian life in myself and in the congregation, and when I had to defend the Lord Jesus Christ against the dishonoring accusation that he had permitted his life to die in the church or had been unable, with the exception of a brief apostolic period, to bring it out of its swaddling clothes or to nurture it to youthful flowering or adult maturity.

According to the apostolic scriptures we assume that "faith, hope, and love" are the spiritual and eternal content of the Christian life, but as long as we cannot differentiate between "these three" according to heathen, Jewish, or Christian speech, nor distinguish between everyday and Sunday understanding, we cannot demonstrate clear expressions of life and clear signs of life, which are peculiar to Christianity. All postulates about Christian life therefore seem to be arbitrary. They seem to involve us in a confused polemic about what is spiritual and what is physical in human life, and about the relationship which Christianity, according to the witness of experience, has to that which the human spirit calls spiritual.

We must discover the Christian expressions of the life of faith in the three ways: in the confession of faith at baptism, in the Christian hope as we have it in the Lord's Prayer at baptism as well as at Communion, and in the love expressed in Christ's word of submission to his faithful or his declaration of love to his bride, the church, in Communion. Only then can we, in our congregational life, show a Christian confession, proclamation, and praise which are the peculiar and unmistakable signs of the Christian faith, the Christian hope, and the Christian love. Then we can speak clearly and judge thoroughly about their relation to faith, hope, and love.

The Christian life in itself will undoubtedly continue to be a profound mystery to us, but the same is true of our total human life, which is separate from that of animals, for no one can make the Christian life known except through comparable spiritual expressions. If someone should object that the Christian signs of life, such as confession, proclamation, and praise, are only words and not action, then we rightly answer that the invisible spirit of man as well as of God can demonstrate its life only through that invisible word which can be heard by the ear and felt in the heart. Every action, by the hand and by all visible things, is vaguely related to the invisible spirit, and we can only glimpse the relationship through a word of enlightenment. Even then we will see darkly in a vague and ambiguous way. The perfect Christian love will seek to express itself in a marvelous generosity and bodily sacrifice, but even the apostolic letter gives testimony that we can give all we own to the poor and we can give our body to be burned and still not have Christian love. It is also evident that many people have done these things without calling themselves Christian or desiring even to be Christians. Even the most dedicated works of love can only be signs of Christian love when they are clearly related to the Christian confession and the Christian song of praise.

This is the outward significance of enlightenment about "the

Christian signs of life"; the significance inward and upward is even more important for all of us. We seek in vain to probe the mysteries of the Christian life, whether it be the mystery of the call in preaching the gospel (the cry of the Christmas message), or the mystery of nurture in the Supper. But the Christian way of life does become brighter and easier for us when we discover the company in which we can seek and expect the Christian faith, the Christian hope, and the Christian love, so that faith is strengthened, hope expanded, and love increased. By this we are furthermore comforted about the gap between the shape of the Christian life in the congregation of the present day and the shape in which it is described by the apostles, in part in themselves and the first fruits of the congregation, but especially in Jesus Christ with fullness and purity. We are comforted not as bookworms who depend on the perfection of an alien life whose description they devour but as a bright boy is comforted about the distance between himself and his adult brother or his aging father. When we are turned aright in our living consideration of the Christian life as a spiritual human life, which is just as real and a lot more human than our physical life, then, like the apostle Paul, we are not anxious about our distance from the goal. Then we see that the Christian life begins with a real conception according to the will of the Spirit, and as the Lord says, with a real birth by water and the Spirit. Then it continues, as did the Lord himself, to grow in age and wisdom and favor with God and man. Then, like Paul, we will strive to forget what is behind us in favor of what is ahead, and by living progress we will reach for the wreath and the crown.

When we regard the Christian life, as also the human life, the mind tells us that there is light behind us but darkness ahead. We can understand no more of life than what we have experienced. On the Christian lifeway, however, there is an unusual and even superhuman light. The Lord has said that whosoever follows after him shall never be in darkness, for he is the true light of the world. The lantern that guides us through the darkness is, as the apostle writes, a sure word of prophecy, which is known by the fact that it corresponds to the Rule of Faith and mankind's sure foundation.

It is a necessary consequence of the covenant of baptism that the spiritual life to which we are born in baptism can in no way be demonic. In every way that spiritual life has to be divine. Christianity presupposes very clearly that human life in the image of God can only be reborn and renewed by a wondrous separation from devildom. How much of humanity is devildom and how much a person has to contribute during his lifetime to the release from deviltry and to the growth of divinity is a puzzle for the mind that can be solved only by experience, and it is no wonder that independent efforts to analyze and determine this matter have led to confusion. The more we listen to the description of the scribes of what is called the "order of salvation," how Scripture calls for us to shed the old man and put on the new, the less we understand the matter. We experience a boundless confusion where it seems as if all of human life must be eradicated as deviltry, or contrariwise as if there was no deviltry, so that man should either direct the new Christian life or stand beside it as an idle observer.

When a person is a living Christian, even when he has not come of age, he realizes that none of the alternatives is true. If there were no devil, no Satan, no Father of Lies, no man of darkness, no murdering angel, if he had no power over man, there would be no word of truth in the gospel of Christ, not an iota of truth in the message about the Son of God as the savior of the world from the power of sin, darkness, and death. For this power can exist and be active only in an unclean spirit of the world. If, on the other hand, all of human nature had become demonic at the Fall, the Son of God could have become a real human being as little as he could have become a devil. Then the new man could not have been wrought in God's image through a rebirth and a renewal of the old man but only by a brand new creation entirely independent of the old man. How the very complicated matter of sanctification and salvation can take place in fallen and sinful humanity, corporately as well as individually, is hidden from our eyes. The Son of God became man in all respects; he was like us but without sin. His life as man cannot demonstrate for us now the new man, who grows up, is liberated from sin and Satan by being cleansed from the "defilement of body and spirit" [2 Cor. 7:1]. If we are to know this, the spirit of truth as the spirit of our Lord Jesus Christ must reveal it for us. But, inasmuch as we, during the growth of the new man, cannot dispense with the tentative knowledge of the growth of life, the spirit of the Lord will also inform us about this when we pray. For it is written about this same spirit: "He will declare to you the things that are to come" [John 16:13]. When it still does not happen the reason must be that the church's faith in the Holy Spirit is either so shaky or so vague that he cannot be called upon or distinguished from the spirits of delusion. Inasmuch as we have only recently gained a sure and definite belief in the Holy Spirit as a divine part of the Trinity, and inasmuch as we have thereby discovered the nature of that "confession" of the incarnate Jesus Christ upon which the spirit of truth can and shall be distinguished from the spirit of delusion, we have only now received the revelation of the Spirit concerning the usefulness for the whole congregation that we keep the faith, fight, and win the crown. This happened when we placed our trust in the confession of faith at baptism as a word to us from the mouth of the Lord.

[In the next three paragraphs Grundtvig shows how this discovery is down to earth and simple, how it fosters a life of faith, and how this life of faith develops from a childlike faith through the seasons of personal growth akin to the seasons of growth in nature.]

It is furthermore a very ordinary bit of human information that the human life which is to be raised is the same life which is under the Fall. The same prodigal son who was lost was the one who was found. He who was dead became alive. The same sheep that was lost was carried home on the shoulder of the shepherd. In the same manner the new man is, strictly speaking, not any other man than the old man. He is only another person in the same sense that Saul became another person when he was anointed and the Spirit came upon him. It is quite clear that God's Son acquired the old mankind when he came to earth as the offspring of a woman, of Abraham's seed and David's seed. Even the new human body of the resurrection was basically the same as the body that was nailed to the cross. Yet, all the scribes who stressed the Christian life as that of our Lord Jesus Christ and no one else have more or less cut the so-called new human life in Christ and his church off from the old human life, as if the latter was a physical life of sin which had to be destroyed and eradicated in order that the new and entirely different human life could succeed it.   This basic error led not only to all the monastic rules but also to all the orthodox dogmatics books, in which the total and basic depravity and spiritual incompetence for doing good was made the foundation for the work of reconciliation. This was claimed, even though it was clearly evident that the human life which was in the need of salvation, of reconciliation, of rebirth and renewal according to the image of the creator would be destroyed.   The consequences were that the old human life, which was given up, daily went to the devil, while the new life either was nothing at all or had no power or was utterly useless except for the purpose of writing dogmatics and memorizing them.   Or else the new spiritual life became inhuman, a demonic life, which battled against humanity and, under all sorts of aliases, raised to the skies that opinionated self-righteousness which always had been characteristic of Satan, the murderer of human life. . . .

It is finally a common human and even evangelical truth that God and his Spirit treat us the same way they want us to treat our neighbor.   This means that we must conquer evil by good, and this is, even by human experience, the only way in which evil is profoundly overcome, driven out, and replaced.   Even the law of God, which can crush the proudest human being with thunder and lightning, cannot eradicate evil desire and lust.   These yield only to the desires of goodness, of which evil desire is a distorted image.   Pride is driven out of the heart only by humility; sensuality, which is impure love, only by pure love; and covetousness for the glories of this world is driven out only by a sincere desire for the glories of God's kingdom.   But I know of no Christian moralist since the days of the apostles who has described the Holy Spirit in this light and spirit.   Such moralists began like the mystics, in the heart, and thus they began in the darkness of the old man which was to be reborn and was to nurture himself with his own love to God and the neighbor.   The result was a false and unreal Christianity from beginning to end.   Or they began with the law, not as a mirror but as a living force and power which was to demolish the pagan temple and out of its ruins erect the temple of the Holy Spirit.   This was done despite the testimony of the Lord that when sanctification begins from without the result will be a tomb filled with filth and dead bones. This was done despite the fact of human experience that when sanctification begins from within we can put on the whole armor of the law and combat the tiniest evil desire until doomsday without moving it one whit. Christian life in the world is always a life of faith and thereby spiritual and invisible, but inasmuch as our physical conduct is open and visible, the Christian church and all its members must, as the apostle writes, use the compulsion of the law, be it the law of Moses or Danish law, to regulate its conduct. If we wish to live a Christian life, we must guard against a sanctification of our legal conduct. We must also guard against the temptation to change the gospel to a new Christian law, which is to compel the soul to a Christian way of thinking and the heart to a Christian life of love. When we try to do this, we either know nothing about Christian living or we squander it, for we can neither be saved nor sanctified by the law without falling from grace.

The tangled knot of Christian living as a life of faith is seen already in all of the letters of Paul. From the very beginning this knot has if not strangled the Christian life among non-Jewish Christians then stunted its growth. It has caused that malady which has been obvious since the days of the apostles. Inasmuch as this knot can be untied only at the resurrection of the body from the dead or by a transformation of the body of the living people who wait for the visible return of the Lord, it is important not to try to cut the knot but to live with it in faith as a thorn in the flesh and to be content with the grace of God whose "power is made perfect in weakness" [2 Cor. 12:9].

Even when we hold fast to the faith that the Christian spiritual life, to which we are reborn in baptism and in which we are nurtured at the Supper, is truly an eternal life, we must yet give up the idea that we can become clearly aware of the Christian life's eternal nature in this world. This is so, because it is only in perfect unity with the Lord and his church that this clear awareness can arise, but also because the awareness is impossible except when "the inner becomes outward," when all the senses and the body functions become as spiritual as the Word of faith, hope, and love is spiritual on our lips and in our hearts. Our whole body must become an eternally pleasing habitation, a perfect tool, and a clear, unblemished mirror of the spirit, the divine power which came from the Father in order to begin and complete the good works in all of our Lord's church. This work will be completed only on the Day of our Lord Jesus Christ, and it will work toward this end in us only when we really denounce ourselves, give up spiritual independence, and willingly let the Holy Spirit, as a divine person, guide our heart and our tongue.   Then we may have the renewed, divine power of living, which alone can create, maintain, and nurture the new humanity in the divine image of Jesus Christ.

Basic Christian Teachings
The Innate and the Reborn Humanity

A monkey needs only to rise on its hind legs when it is dressed up and taught to imitate our human ways. Then it is said that the monkey is as human as many people we know. As long as this is true, it is futile to speak or write about the real humanity, be it the childlike innate life from our mother's womb or the childlike reborn life to which we are given birth in the Lord's baptism, the baptism of water and the Spirit. Even when we become aware that the difference between mankind and dumb creatures lies in words and speech, the true nature of man is yet obscured if we regard words to be only sounds. These would not differ from roars and barks or even from imitations such as can be taught to magpies and parrots.

Only when we become aware that human speech on our tongue and lips can and must be a marvelous something, a matchless gift which no bird or animal can be taught to imitate, only then are we qualified to consider humanity and the various stages in which this life is revealed to us. We must call this life created and divine, for this is our common bond and therefore our bond with our common and invisible creator, God. Then we discover with ease that human words and human speech have a threefold character which is peculiar to them. They have three qualities which separate them from cackling and parroting, namely, power, truth, and love. These qualities may vary, but some degree of each must be found in speech which is called human. When we find no force, vigor, or willfulness in so-called speech, we call it empty and dead; when we find no truth, we call it false and dishonest; and when we find no love, we call it inhuman and heartless.

When we have established that humanity has its only forceful expression, its certain goals, its clear image in human speech with a higher invisible power, a profound truth, and an unlimited love, then we have the standpoint from which it can and must be judged. It will then be evident, of course, that innate and reborn humanity are as far apart as the quality, the width, and the degree of those higher life-powers called truth and love and goodness with which humanity expresses itself in speech.   On the other hand, it is always the same humanity which we consider, with the same laws, the same original character, the same vital powers and criteria.   Human life in its most obscure, most poverty-stricken and uncleanest form is nevertheless of the same kind of human life in its richest, purest, and most clarified shape.   In one word, the malefactor on the cross had the same humanity as the only-begotten Son of God, our Lord Jesus Christ, to whom he cried, "Lord, remember me when you come in your kingdom!" and from whom he received the honest, forceful, and loving answer, "Verily I say to you, today you shall be with me in paradise."

If this were not so, the possibility of God's only Son becoming a real, human child, born of a woman, would be no greater than the possibility of a woman-born human child becoming a child of God, born of water and the Spirit.   Then divinity would have excluded humanity and in return humanity would have excluded divinity. There could then have been no talk of a hearty, spiritual mutuality, inclination, and interaction.   It is therefore awkwardly true when Mohammedan theologians deny the incarnation and the fusion of two natures in the personality of our Lord Jesus Christ, for they have always agreed with Mohammed and the Koran in declaring that the divine and the human natures are so different that no contact was possible.   Consequently, they also reject the possibility of the work of redemption.   They ultimately reject divine revelation to mankind and any response to human prayer.   The minor falsehoods flow from the primary one.   If man is not created in the image of God, he could not have fallen into sin and could not have been reborn.   He could not even think truly and in a living manner about God, his Word, and his kingdom.

It is evidently inconsistent, argumentative, and extremely boring when so-called Catholic or Protestant theologians, evangelical or biblical, admit and insist on the creation of man in the image of God and the renewal in the same image by faith in the Son of God and the Son of man, our Lord Jesus Christ, when with equal vigor they insist that "the Fall," which occurred between creation and renewal and which makes the reconciliation or renewal indispensable for salvation, has distorted, or rather erased, the life in God's image and destroyed mankind, so that there is nothing left of the created glory or the relation to God.   Consequently, all that Mohammedan theologians say about fallen man as well as about the entire nature of mankind would be true.   Then the story of revelation and the whole work of reconciliation become a series of impossibilities which must be surmounted by the dead and powerless written word that whatever is impossible for man is possible for God.

I call this written word dead and powerless because it is only in its dead and powerless literalness that it seems to surmount the impossibilities.   As soon as this Word of the Lord becomes spirit and life for us, we see immediately that what this word means and what it can and will eliminate are only the essential impossibilities (*adynata*), for these are impossibilities only when omnipotence is absent.   In no way, however, can or will this word eliminate the alleged impossibilities, which should really be called impracticabilities or unmentionables, which neither God nor man can perform without self-contradiction.   If, in regard to this matter, we still insist that God should perform what was impossible for man, we would mock both God and the truth; the voice of God and consciousness of truth, which we call our conscience, would have to revolt.   The word which is in our mouth and in our heart would then obviously be denied all facility for expressing spiritual and eternal truths, unless the only accessible truth for man would be that there was no spiritual and eternal truth, or that truth was not true to itself, so that falsehood was truth.

[Grundtvig continues this argument for two more pages which add nothing to our illumination.   The method of his argumentation is obviously that of the Principle of Contradiction, a principle of logic adhered to by eighteenth-century Enlightenment and which was taught to both Grundtvig and Kierkegaard at the University of Copenhagen in the form of Christian Wolff's teaching. A feature of the Principle is that when you are faced with two alternatives you can prove the one by disproving the other.]

All of the so-called Bible history can be true as a divine history of revelation only when we assume that humanity is similar and the same before and after the Fall as well as before and after the rebirth. If Adam's humanity in the image of God had been destroyed by the Fall, God could not address the fallen Adam nor could Adam answer him. Still less could Abraham, the child of Adam, be called the friend of God; nor could God speak to Moses, a child of Adam, as a man speaks to his neighbor; nor could the spirit of God rest on other children of Adam, such as Samuel, David, the prophets, and John the Baptist. God could not use the voice of man to speak to men or touch their hearts. Adam's kin would be bewitched or demonized and would be made into an animal or a demon, an unnatural changeling composed of animality and demonism, who could neither be saved from anything nor to anything. As the children of the devil have always claimed, this makes sense only when one assumes that human existence was part of the hellish punishment and confinement placed upon the fallen angels. The Egyptians told us this when they claimed that the gods, fearing Typhon and his thunder[18] sought refuge among the animals.

If we then assume, as Holy Writ and our Savior Jesus Christ, born of woman, assumed, that it is the life of Adam and Eve in the image of God that was transplanted to the Savior as the "seed of the woman," despite the Fall and its awful consequences, and if we assume that he is the Second Adam and the New Man, cleansed, reconciled to God, and resurrected to a new and justified life, then we must also consider the new Christian, human life in the congregation of our Lord as the same humanity, originating in Adam, propagated through Eve, fallen, plundered, ill-treated, and corrupted by the Evil One in all of us, but raised from the Fall, saved, made whole, and divinely equipped in Christ. In baptism this life is continuously reborn in the Christian congregation, so that the Christian rebirth and renewal of humanity in all of us presupposes

18. Typhon is a mythological monster.

the Holy Spirit and originates through him out of the old humanity. This old humanity is the only human womb for new life, and, like Eve, it could not decline so far nor be so impoverished or corrupted that it could not find the grace of God and give birth to the children of the most high.   As it is spoken by the prophet: "Shall I, who cause to bring forth, shut the womb?" [Isa. 66:9].

This plan of God, which necessarily seems obscure to us, has a new light cast upon it when we consider the Word, which is with God and with man, to be not only a means of revelation but also the exclusive expression of spiritual life.   The Word is the light of life, even as Scripture says that "whatsoever doth make manifest is light" [Eph. 5:13 KJV], and that the Word "that enlightens every man was coming into the world" [John 1:9], but the Word which is with man is both the divine image of life and the divine image of light in which God created man.

From this insight it follows that in the human word about the invisible, the spiritual, and the eternal life we can trace the involvement and development of man.   We can trace the Fall with all its sad and corrupted fruits and we can trace the resurrection of life with all its joyful and blessed fruits.   We are never tempted to underrate the corruption of life in the sign and the perdition of death, but neither are we tempted to underrate the value of the Word as the unifying and continuing factor of life.   Light is thus shed upon the tongues of all peoples in their relation to the new Christian life, and new tongues as of fire will rest upon them as the spirit gives them utterance to proclaim the great acts of God each in his own native language [see Acts 2].

This is an important insight into the fact that humanity and the human word are inseparable.   It is the necessary presupposition for all sound consideration of a Word of God as an impingement upon human life.   When we speak as human beings about divine revelation, its impression upon the human heart and its expression in human speech, we are speaking about an insight that is more human than it is actually Christian.   This insight is concerned about the relation between God and man, or between spirit and dust, and it can be considered to precede Christianity.   Inasmuch, however, as the Christian revelation is actually the "incarnation of the Word," and inasmuch as Christian worship in spirit and truth is the Christian yet physical acceptance and utterance of the Word (hearing through the ear and confessing with the mouth), the insight into the nature of the Word must necessarily come from the Christian life of human beings, and it is completely indispensable for the full development, growth, and explanation of humanity.

Insight into the nature of the Word has been investigated and exhausted in the ancient Greek church and it has been expressed as a Logos-science or a Christo-logy.[19] This is an obscure and complicated matter, hard to explain and therefore without much benefit. It is invaluable, however, in the knowledge and clarification of the matter, to consider historically the life of the Word in relation to the languages of God's people, particularly of our own people, and I will therefore direct the attention of all enlightened Christians to this.

It would be too elaborate to consider both the Hebrew and the Danish languages in this connection and to compare their facility for expressing "spiritual things with spiritual" [1 Cor. 2:13 KJV], and I shall postpone this to another time. I would like in closing, however, in a general way, to give information about the grossly misunderstood connection between folk-life and Christianity by calling attention to the inseparable relation between the language of a people and its inner nature, its mode of expression and its development. . . .

[In three paragraphs Grundtvig discusses language and words in details which are difficult to transfer to English and which do not add to the argument for us.]

It would be unspiritual and awkward to banish or even eradicate the old, original humanity in order to give room to a new Christian humanity, but it would be just as unspiritual and awkward to banish and eradicate folk-life and replace it with Christianity. If we should say to the spirit of a people: Depart, thou unclean spirit and give room to the Holy Spirit!, then we could be rid of the folk spirit, but this would be no guarantee that it would be replaced by the Holy Spirit. It might exclude all spirits in this people, all spiritual influence and intuition, all spiritual and profound understanding and insight.

19. The Greek word for "word" is *logos.*

Basic Christian Teachings
The Word of Eternal Life from the
Mouth of the Lord to the Church

[Grundtvig concludes "Basic Christian Teachings" with a lengthy, 266-page, treatise under the above title. It is too long and repetitious to include in this volume. Most of the material and argumentation are covered in other writings, and the approach in this treatise is largely historical, i.e., the history of the church and the history of his own experience. We have therefore selected only three passages.]

The fact that the Word from the mouth of the Lord is spoken to all of us at baptism and Communion is the one true foundation for the faith of all Christians, old and young, wise and uninformed. This Word from the mouth of the Lord is the foundation for light and life; it is the rock and the sun, enlightening and enlivening in the spirit of the Lord, which never deviates from what he has said. The Holy Scriptures are means of information. The Scriptures are not mentioned by the Lord and they do not contain the confession of faith which the church uses at baptism. They are the tools of the Spirit and the scholars, and they are given freedom of influence on the condition that the scholars use them in a Christian manner, in accord with the Christian faith that is obvious to all. There must be a free interchange between the emancipated congregation of the Lord and the scholars, and the latter may never present their insights as articles of faith.

* * * *

I have always only toyed with the scraps of paper which dignified scholars place on the scales to counteract the unanimous witness of the church at baptism in continuous succession from generation to generation, from baptism to baptism. Even the writings of Irenaeus or Eusebius do not weigh more than a goose quill in com-

parison with the ancient and solemn testimony of the free congregation at baptism in regard to the faith.   In the churches of compulsion, however, with their priesthoods and their ritual, this basic
relationship has been so concealed, overlooked, and obscured that in
my lifelong career I have not been able to make even professors
understand that when I refer to the confession of faith at baptism of
the ancient church I am referring to the audible "Yes—Amen!" of
the congregation.   I am not, as Lessing does, referring to ancient
recordings of the so-called *Symbolum Apostolicum* or other utterances
about the confession in the writings of the so-called fathers.

* * * *

Christian enlightenment proceeds from the proposition that the
entire creation and temporal existence has its origin in the eternal
"Word of God," which was with God and was God and which is the
light of man.   Similarly, the Christian enlightenment as well as the
Christian life and history proceed from the spiritual fact that the
"Word of God" became flesh in the fullness of time in order to
gather a faithful congregation which lives in a hearty fellowship with
him.   This congregation derives its spirit from his spirit, its flesh
from his flesh, and it must therefore be the aim of all Christian
enlightenment to show how all temporal things have their original
coherence in the Word of God from eternity, and to show how, in
the course of time, all things have cohered in Christ Jesus and how
they live and move in his congregation [John 1; Eph. 4; Col. 1].

SERMONS

Translated by
ENOK MORTENSEN

N. F. S. Grundtvig as a Preacher

by Enok Mortensen

No selection of the writings of Grundtvig would be complete without a sampling of his sermons. It should be evident from other
selections in this volume that Grundtvig was not only an educator,
an historian, and a poet; he was also a devout Christian and an
ordained parish pastor, and it is impossible to understand his views
on history and education apart from his concept of God and the
Christian church.

Grundtvig's first sermon was preached in 1810 and he preached
his last sermon September 1, 1872, the day before his death.
Through forty-seven years he had preached virtually every Sunday
and on other holidays, and most of his notes for more than three
thousand sermons are preserved. His first published volume of
sermons, *Bibelske Praedikener* (Biblical Sermons) appeared in 1816.
As recently as 1974 the Danish theologian P. G. Lindhardt has
published *Konfrontation*,[20] a selection of sermons on the background
of Grundtvig's reaction to Søren Kierkegaard's attack on official
Christendom, during 1854-55, and some of the quotations below
are from this volume.

It is possible that readers today will find his sermons wordy and
dull, but it must be remembered that styles of preaching have
changed considerably since Grundtvig's time. As a regularly appointed pastor he followed the prescribed pericopes, and his sermons
were biblical and thematic. He usually interpreted texts allegori-
cally and his preaching was directed toward the congregation not to
the world at large.

While other writings of Grundtvig reflect an appreciation of
man's "simple, joyful, and active life on earth," most of his sermons,
ironically enough, are pietistically molded and they differentiate

20. P. G. Lindhardt, *Konfrontation* (Copenhagen, 1974).

sharply between "the saved," i.e., the Christian community, and "the world," i.e., the unbelievers.   Yet Grundtvig was neither a puritan nor a pessimist. He believed firmly in God's continuing creation and the power of God's grace and the Holy Spirit to heal the wounds of suffering, sin, and death.   In contrast to Lutheran orthodoxy, which had considered the Bible the sole norm and source for Christian faith, Grundtvig emphasized the Apostles' Creed at baptism as the Christian's confession of faith.   Still, Grundtvig considered himself a true disciple of Luther, and the first sermon in this collection is in reality a Reformation sermon reflecting his great admiration for Martin Luther.   The sermon for the 18th Sunday after Trinity, 1845, underscores the Johannine emphasis on Jesus Christ as the Living Word.

The last four sermons offered in this volume contain references to Søren Kierkegaard's vitriolic attacks on the official church, his charge that "the Christianity of the New Testament doesn't exist," and that pastors, instead of enduring poverty, suffering, and death, have "vast incomes, honor and esteem, and worldly pleasures." Grundtvig does not mention Kirkegaard by name, but his Palm Sunday sermon of 1855 is obviously a refutation of Kierkegaard's attack.   The mention of "barrels of gold" may be a reference to the enormous wealth Kierkegaard himself was alleged to possess, but Grundtvig insists, scoffers to the contrary, that disciples are not called upon to flee the world but to live in it, sustained by "the Lord's word which is spirit and life."

The same theme is continued in his Good Friday sermon. Grundtvig admits that we have not taken up our cross or reached Christian perfection, but he boldly challenges "the unreasonable and un-Christian allegation that we are not true Christians because we have not reached Christian perfection," for the word of the Cross is living among us, and eventually it will manifest itself in the life of the church.

The sermon on the 8th Sunday after Trinity is a refutation of Kierkegaard's charge that state-appointed pastors were false prophets.   Grundtvig maintains that it is an impossible demand that Christians, in order to do God's will, must deny themselves and conquer the world, for the Christian life "is by no means, as the false prophets proclaim, a life of constant sorrow and anguish, pain and plague, for such was not the life our Lord Jesus Christ himself lived on earth." His life, in spite of adversities, was still in its totality "the most joyful, the most blissful human life that has been and can be lived in this world."

In the last sermon, the 4th Sunday after Easter, 1855, Grundtvig sees the church and the world as being in "a great transition period," but he is firm in his conviction that the church shall receive "the fullness of the spiritual riches which we have in earthly vessels."

All Saints' Day
1839

Holy God and Father! Thy Word is truth! Thy Word is life and spirit, the Word of faith which must be heard. Yes, heavenly Father, thou who until now so wondrously has preserved and, when it seemed dead, through thy Holy Spirit again has quickened thy salvatory Word, O let it never die in our hearts and in the hearts of our children, but live among us from generation to generation and grow through thy Son, our Lord Jesus Christ, to thy glory and praise, and to our salvation! Our Father, who art in heaven!

"The earth was without form and void, and darkness was upon the face of the deep; and the Spirit of God was moving over the face of the waters. And God said, 'Let there be light'; and there was light. And God saw that the light was good." [Gen. 1:2-4]

These well-known words from the book of Genesis may rightly be applied to the days of Martin Luther and to God's great deeds in and with him whom we are gathered to commemorate with joy and gratitude today!

Yes, my friends, the earth was in truth without form and void for the hearts who rejected this world and desired a commonwealth in heaven. For them the earth was more formless and empty than it had ever been since the Baptizer rose up and the Savior came down; since the host of angels proclaimed to God's people tidings of great joy, and the Word of eternal life on the lips of the Son of Man reached toward the ends of the earth. For a long time this true Word of God had been infiltrated by so much human learning, so many fables and dreams, that it was difficult to recognize it; but as long as there was life in the dreams about all God's saints who hovered about their enshrined bones and who proclaimed their saintliness with signs and wondrous deeds—life in the fabulous dream

88

about the holy sepulcher where the Lord had lain, and angels descending and ascending with consolation for the penitent who knelt at the holy places, bringing their prayers to the throne of God—as long as there was life in these dreams, people were bewitched as by the evening glow of the day which had brought the glow of dawn from on high. But the hour of delusion had passed; darkness with all its horror had struck. The earth was without form and void, and darkness was upon the face of the deep.

For the earth is indeed without form and void in a spiritual sense when the Word about the earth's relationship to heaven—the word about the way to the land of the living—has been silenced or chilled to the point of petrification, rendering it dead and incapacitated. Thus it was at the time when Martin Luther appeared. The word of the Lord was scarce in those days, and the sun had set on the prophets who had said, "I have dreamed, I have dreamed!" [Jer. 23:25]. There were no longer visions or songs, and all prophetic scriptures were like a book given to someone unable to read, or a sealed book no one could open.

Not only Christianity but also everything else which innately had exalted the spirit of the peoples and warmed their hearts had become dead and impotent. And the affliction was by no means caused by a scarcity of Bibles or other famous books, for through the invention of the printing press they were now easier to find and to possess. But when the living and powerful word, which the Creator has laid on the lips of man, is silenced, so that heartwarming and eloquent speech deals only with silver and gold and precious stones, eating and drinking, buffoonery and vanity, gambling and dancing and carnal pleasures, or with spears and swords, murder and manslaughter, raging revenge, and sly wiles—then all prophetic scriptures, both God's and man's, dealing with both heights and depths, have become like a closed book no one can open, or an open book no one can read.

Yes, in such spiritless and lifeless times Martin Luther was born and grew up. And there was darkness upon the face of the deep, on the brink of which mortals either sighed and wept, either danced or roared; darkness over the abyss to which death is the door and the tomb a symbol; but darkness first and last within ourselves: the

monstrous bottomless emptiness into which human souls sink and
are lost, feeling themselves cast away from the face of God, exiled
from the land of the living and bereft of all consolation and joy.
There was darkness over the abyss and it was not, as it is sometimes
said, merely the darkness of superstition but much more that of
unbelief.   For there was no lack of people who, to their own way of
thinking, were as clever, as captivated by their own reason and
intelligence, as anyone can be.   Also, there was no lack in many
lands of people who had read many books and who knew them by
rote, so that if few people knew the Bible it was only, then as now,
because they cared not for its content.   Nor, finally, was there a lack
of artists of all kinds who fashioned beautiful and costly objects
which are still highly praised.   And if those who bought letters of
indulgence from monks and priests, popes, and bishops, were
superstitious, then those who sold these objects for ready cash were
yet more unbelieving, and they ridiculed among themselves not only
the superstition by which they made a living but also the faith which
was thus dishonored.

Thus the earth was without form and void because among
thousands one hardly found one, and that one a mute, who cared
about things above.   And there was darkness on the face of the deep
because they who saw it assiduously covered it with conjured darkness.   But the Spirit of God still moved over the face of the waters
wherever the covenant had been kept by those who baptized in the
name of the Father and the Son and the Holy Spirit.   Yes, precisely
in areas where the papacy bore down on souls as a heavy yoke and
made itself felt as darkness over the abyss, precisely there and there
alone, the Spirit of God moved over the waters, in baptism.   And
therefore it was not an angel who descended from heaven and rolled
back the stone from the tomb, nor a prophet from other parts of the
world using his speech to dispel the darkness from the abyss.   No, it
was, as we know, a monk who as an infant in swaddling clothes had
been brought to the Lord, who took him in his arms, blessing him
and saying, "The Lord is with thee, go in peace!"   Yes, to him in
his monk's cage the Lord said, " 'Let there be light'; and there was
light."

Yes, my friends, Martin Luther felt the emptiness, found himself on the brink of the abyss over which the darkness brooded, and he detached himself from the world and fled to the monastery, which the serious-minded considered the only place one might escape the abyss and with repentance and penance save one's soul. There he sat sorrowing night and day; he read and prayed and tormented his soul, but found neither light nor peace; for it simply is not true that it was by reading he found peace. No, he believed in the Lord Jesus though he did not know him and was unaware of his goodness. And the Lord Jesus, who in baptism had made a covenant with him, fulfilled in him the words of the gospel for today, "Blessed are the poor in spirit, for theirs is the kingdom of heaven. Blessed are those who mourn, for they shall be comforted" [Matt. 5:3-4].

Yes, my friends, never has any mortal spoken in such a way on the strength of his own spirit, for who except a scoffer can declare that those who mourn are blessed, unless he is able to give them comfort and solace? But that the Lord Jesus both could and would do this—no less after fifteen hundred years following his ascension than when he declared to his disciples, " 'Peace be with you!' and breathing upon them, 'Receive the Holy Spirit!' "—this Luther learned in the monastery from an old monk, whom the Lord had detained, like the ancient Simeon, in order to see his salvation and a light for revelation to the Gentiles. For when the old monk saw that Luther sorrowed for God and that it was his sins that overwhelmed and crushed him to the ground, he had compassion on him, searched his own heart for a buried treasure, and opened the sealed lips with the secret of the gospel, "Brother Martin, believe that the Lord Jesus has made full satisfaction for your sins, just as I believe he has done for me, and you will have peace." With these words a light was lit for Luther, a light over the abyss and glory to him who brings souls therefrom. And God saw that the light was good; for it was his own Word with life and light, it was the light which had shone in the darkness, though the darkness comprehended it not [John 1:5 KJV].

Yes, my friends, "finished" was the last word the Savior uttered from the cross before he bowed his head and yielded up his spirit, and this "finished" is the word by which God creates light in the darkness of the soul from generation to generation. That light is good, because it is the true light of the world, Jesus Christ himself, the Lord, our light, our salvation, and our power of life!

Luther still sorrowed, sorrowed all his days, but not without hope and consolation, and less for himself than for the millions who sat in darkness and the shadow of death without seeing the great light which had dawned when the old sun darkened, the great light emanating from the God-given Word, "finished," and risen with him who died for us and shed his blood unto forgiveness of our sins! For those Luther now sorrowed, but only as one who finds the sorrow sweet in the consolation and solace which follows according to the Lord's word—in its fullness only when he rests in the bosom of Abraham, but also here, more often than mortal clay can figure and sweeter than our lips can tell.

Yes, my friends, God saw that the light was good, and Luther saw it; but our forefathers also saw it. Many people saw it and praised God who had given us such a man, had raised a great prophet among us, and had visited his people. And Martin Luther rejoiced as the woman who has sorrow because her hour has come, but who no longer remembers the anguish, for joy that a child is born into the world [John 16:21].

Yes, my friends, the light was so good that it spread abroad because it emanated from the Word of Life as the light for the living. Luther saw that only a living word in their own mother tongue could enlighten the peoples about God's great deeds; and the light placed such a living word on his lips for his people. God placed a new song in his mouth which gladdened the hearts and became a living word also on the lips of our forefathers in our mother tongue. This was not, as is usually alleged, because the Holy Scriptures were translated into Luther's and into our own native language, as well as others. The living word emanated not from the Book, but the word cast light upon the book so that the book was known by the Lord's light as a work by his Spirit and a masterly picture of him and his house, the house of living stones: his believing church.

Yes, my friends, let us join our forefathers in praise that the light, which dawned for Luther, was good and was communicated through words from his lips to those who heard him; for the light was Jesus

Christ who accompanies his word from mouth to mouth and from heart to heart until the close of the age. Let us perceive and proclaim that through the dawning of that light a new creation began, a new day in Christendom, a creation through which not only the darkness upon the face of the deep was dispersed, but the earth which had been without form and void became bright and alive with the sun, moon, and stars above the firmament, with grass and flowers and all sorts of trees, with birds in the air and fish in the sea, with all kinds of animals, and finally man in God's image and after his likeness!

Let it not diminish our joy, but rather enhance it and our thanksgiving, that once again a period arrived when the earth was without form and void and with darkness upon the face of the deep. For it was evident that this was only a night between the days of creation, evening and morning before our eyes. Or it was as a winter's night superseded by a morn in spring in which we shall rejoice with the birds and look forward to behold the deeds of God toward which he graciously has called us to be co-workers.

Yes, let us thank God for Martin Luther who brought a dawn, this new Abraham, our father in Christ. Let those who now preach the gospel proclaim that word "finished," which creates light for our souls and peace with God in our hearts, so that they may join the Lord in saying that blessed are those who mourn in his house, for they shall be comforted with heavenly sweetness. May this father of our church, also of our children and grandchildren, become a father until the Lord comes in the glory of his Father, whom Martin Luther encouraged us to call upon freely in the name of him who healed our infirmities and bore our pains, in the blessed name of our Lord and Savior Jesus Christ! Amen!

18th Sunday after Trinity
1845

Holy God and Father! Thy Word is truth! Thy Word is spirit and life to us, the Word of faith which must be heard. Yes, heavenly Father, let us always sense more deeply and recognize more clearly what a precious and fruitful treasure we have in thy living Word, which not only reveals to us thy secret counsel toward our salvation but, when we faithfully love and hold it fast, links and unites us with thee through thy lovable, only-begotten Son as coheirs to the glory which is his at thy right hand. Hear our prayer in the name of our Lord Jesus Christ. Our Father, who art in heaven!

"What do you think of the Christ? Whose son is he?" [Matt. 22:42ff.].

Thus, according to the gospel for the day, Christ himself, with divine calmness, asked his enemies who tempted him with the great commandment of the law—the enemies who would know nothing of a Christ but only of one who was the son of David. And we learn that he bound their lips, reminding them of David's words, "The Lord said to my Lord, Sit at my right hand, till I put thy enemies under thy feet." It is in vain, however, that we attempt to muzzle the mouths of the unbelievers today with David's words, not only because they care as little about David's words as about Christ's, but especially because they take lightly all words about spiritual things and do not sense the strength in the Lord's question, "If David thus calls Christ Lord, how is he his son?"

It is of course awkward when the son lords it over the father, and spiritually speaking it is impossible, because the son must either be without spirit or possess the father's spirit. But the scribes and other learned men of the world today are not perceptive enough to see that, for just as they find it entirely natural in daily living that

94

the son lords it over the father, the young over the old, so they apparently ignore their inconsistency in calling Christ lord in the spirit, while still asserting that his servants lord it over him.

I mention this, however, not just to quarrel with the Lord's enemies either about Christ or about the Word, but in order to remind the Lord's friends that Christ and the Word basically are one and the same; for it is written, "And the Word became flesh and dwelt among us" [John 1:14], and again, "That which was from the beginning, which we have heard, which we have seen with our eyes, which we have looked upon and touched with our hands, concerning the word of life . . . we proclaim also to you" [1 John 1:1-3]. This basic oneness of the Word with our Lord Jesus Christ, you see, is not merely a profound truth which sheds light on God's only-begotten Son, through whom he created and redeemed the world, but it is also a blissful secret which gives the believers the blessed assurance that God's Son, their Lord and Savior, is as near to them as in his Word of faith on their lips and in their hearts, and this Word has the power to conquer the world, defy the gates of hell, accomplish the good deeds of the Father, and, above all, raise the dead to life.

But if it is to be light and life for us that Christ and the Word basically and spiritually are one, we must be on guard lest we become tainted by the world's wanton and slovenly ideas not only about Christ but about the Word. For if the Word loses its constancy and firmness for us, then all our so-called faith in Christ and our fellowship with him are in vain. Then it becomes evident that the only name by which we can be saved, the name of Jesus Christ, is also a word that loses its firmness and constancy, just like the others. And it is therefore the great sorrow for us who seriously proclaim the gospel of God's Son, that in the midst of bombastic twaddle about the Spirit, many of Christ's disciples lose their firm confidence in the Word. Their profound respect for it has been shaken and weakened, if not blown away, so that we hardly know how to build a firm foundation which can support the tower which indeed reaches heavenward.

However, just as it is written that we are to build upon the foundation of the apostles and the prophets, Christ Jesus himself being the chief cornerstone, we also read that the prophet said, "I believed, and so I spoke," and the apostle says the same. The Lord himself says, "If you love me, you will keep my commandments" (words) "and I will . . . manifest myself to him" [Eph. 2:20; 2 Cor. 4:13; John 14:15, 21]. We have therefore clearly nothing else to do but to speak tirelessly as we believe, and with all our might exalt the Word of God as the power of God to salvation for everyone who believes, assured that the same spirit of Christ, which compels and strengthens us to do that, can and will also give the Word witness among all those who are of the truth.

Yes, my friends, just as we are convinced that every person's own conscience tells him that in serious matters one must stand by his word lest all assurance disappear concerning intangible things, just so we can and must be confident that the spirit of truth witnesses for all its worshipers. In questions concerning faith and all spiritual matters everything hinges on the Word. If we disassociate ourselves from that and no longer depend on it, the soul is driven hither and yon like a reed in the wind and everything falters under us. For the Word is the spirit's sole revelation and the only barrier between truth and falsehood. When we let go of the Word we rumble in darkness, losing our bearings and unable to resist any temptation. Just as in daily living, then, our security and confidence are based on the trust that we can rely on the words and promises of the people we associate with, just so is the foundation for all firmness in the faith and certainty in hope that we hold fast the Word which reveals and expresses them; for it becomes profitable to ask about truth and credibility only when we hold fast the Spirit and the thought through the Word.

For what would be the use of asking about the truth of Christianity if we did not have a word which proclaimed what Christianity is and what we are to believe and confess in order to be a Christian? And of what use is it to have such a Word in the covenant of baptism if we will not, dare not, hold it fast and believe it? Just as it is meaningless to ask people what they think of Christ when they don't know what we think of Christ, so it is useless to ask whose son Christ is according to our Christian faith if we do not hold fast the Word in the confession of faith, which witnesses that he is the only-begotten Son of God, the Father, or emphasize the word "only-begotten" which sets him apart from other children of God, such as angels or human beings.

Thus we observe in the gospel for today that the Lord emphasized the words "Son" and "Lord" by saying, "If David calls him Lord, how is he the son?" and so we must also emphasize the words "Son" and "Lord" and all the words in the confession of faith in order to know whether we believe or not and whether or not the Christian faith is the true faith.

My friends, if the Word therefore did not have more to do with Christ than it has with the Spirit and all spiritual things, which are revealed only in words and believed because of the Word, then there could be no Christianity without faith in the Word and reverence for it. But since Christ and the Word are one and the same, we see clearly the shrewdness of the Enemy when the world would have us believe that we can retain our Christian faith, our Christian hope, and our Savior's love without the Word, since, says the Enemy, it is only the spirit that gives life.

Yes, my friends, such is the Enemy's shrewd cunning that he uses truth and freedom as tempting sham. Therefore we must be aware that when we relinquish the Word of the Lord we dissociate ourselves from him, and then we must either lose all stability and security or we must bind ourselves to our own words about Christ or those of others—words which completely lack the divine vitality found in the Word of God's Son, when he and the Word, through the Spirit, are one. Then the Enemy shall not seize or deceive us. Then we bind ourselves to the Word of the Lord, not as his slaves but as the friends of him who says, "If a man loves me, he will keep my word, and my Father will love him, and we will come to him" [John 14:23]. We bind ourselves to his Word because we believe that through it he binds himself to us and gives us a grasp of the unshakable truth, a sure token of his Father's love and a holy temple in which he himself will dwell spiritually among us and reveal his glory. As it is written, "And the Word became flesh and dwelt among us, full of grace and truth; we have beheld his glory, glory as of the only Son from the Father" [John 1:14].

Yes, my friends, just let the learned men of the world and the scribes pity and mock us because we are babes who cling to the

Word, too timid through the power of the Spirit to move freely between heaven and earth! From the first moment of our faith we have the consolation from the lips of the Lord that God has revealed to babes what is hidden for the wise and understanding [Matt. 11:25], when we lovingly keep the Word of the Lord in our hearts we soon learn that his Word, as he says, is spirit and life. For long before we glimpse the light revealing the deep secret that he himself is in his Word we sense it in the security we have in the faith, so that we do not ask, " 'Who will ascend into heaven?' (that is, to bring Christ down) or 'Who will descend into the abyss?' (that is, to bring Christ up from the dead)" [Rom. 10:6-7], and we find it divinely affirmed by the power of the Word of the Lord within us and through him to whom God the Father said, "Sit at my right hand, till I make your enemies your footstool!" [Ps. 110:1].

Yes, my friends, that Word of the Lord to which we refer is the confession of faith with the words of institution both at baptism and at the Lord's Supper, including the Lord's Prayer and benediction. This Word cannot dwell a single day in a believing heart and not reign over its enemies, as it is written about the Lord. And these known enemies—conceit with all its doubts and objections, willfullness with all its ungodly lust, and egotism with all its worldly covetousness—are trampled to death daily under the feet of the Word, just as all enemies of the Lord eventually shall be laid under his footstool while the heavens rejoice: the nations of the world belong to the Lord and his Anointed!

All our trust in the Lord Jesus Christ and all our hope of his glory rest in the faith that he sits at the right hand of God, from whence he shall come again to judge the living and the dead. Just so, our faith is enlivened by our belief that the Word of the Lord reigns divinely within us, and only when we thereby learn that the Lord truly is one with his Word can we also clearly perceive that the Lord Jesus Christ reigns in the midst of his enemies and sits at the right hand of God the Father, while all his enemies are placed under his footstool.

Yes, my friends, when the Word of faith (the confession of faith) as it was in the beginning is on our lips and in our hearts, and when we then consider how hostile the world has been, and is, toward this

Word, though it never was refuted or stifled—then we perceive clearly that it has reigned and still reigns in the midst of its enemies. And whenever it victoriously attacked heresy and error, darkness and ignorance, sin and sorrow, and fear of death, it laid enemies under its feet.   Thus it is not only within us but throughout the whole earth where the gospel is preached that the Word of faith with spirit and power proves its oneness with the Lord at God's right hand, because he is the Word of the beginning through whom all things are created and in whom both heavenly and earthly things have their deep coherence.

Therefore, let us rest in this faith in the Word, so that through daily experience we learn that Jesus dwells in our hearts and that there exists also on earth, secretly, a heaven where our Lord and Savior sits at God's right hand and does what he pleases.   Then we shall never fear the world, be deceived by the Enemy's cunning, or doubt that our life, our eternal life, which through Christ is hidden with God, shall be revealed with him in the Father's glory.

Amen!   In the name of our Lord Jesus!   Amen!

Palm Sunday
1855

Father of our Lord Jesus Christ, and our Father! Maker of heaven and earth! Thy Word through thy only Son is truth, spirit, and life, the Word of faith, hope, and love which must be heard, believed, and confessed so that thy good works through thy Holy Spirit can be fulfilled among us until the day of our Lord Jesus Christ. Our Father, who art in heaven!

"The Pharisees then said to one another, . . . 'Look, the world has gone after him'" [John 12:19].

These are the strange words we read in the Gospel of John on the occasion of the Lord's entry into Jerusalem, following the raising of Lazarus, when people by the thousands went to meet him, spread their clothes on the road, and intoned with his disciples, "Hosanna to the Son of David! Blessed is he who comes in the name of the Lord! Hosanna in the highest!" [Matt. 21:9].

The words are strange because they sound again many hundreds of years after the death, resurrection, and ascension of the Lord, sound again each time the multitudes momentarily and voluntarily intone the Christian song of praise, and are then always closest to denying and banishing the Christian faith. In that respect the scoffers need not thus loudly fill our ears; we servants of the Lord are well aware of it, we have always known it, and we have never placed much emphasis on the world's so-called Christianity, which is at the moment the Christian millions, the so-called Christian nations, and all that this implies. Yes, we know more than that, we know that when the Spirit of the Lord has produced its final sign on the earth, corresponding to the Lord's last sign in the days of his flesh by raising Lazarus who had been in the grave four days and was already stinking, then it will, by and large, seem as if the whole world is going after him, but soon thereafter it will be evident that the world no longer tolerates the spirit of the Lord and the name of the Lord among them.

Yes, my friends, such is the world and such it will continue to be. But when scoffers shout that we therefore, if we want permission to call ourselves Christian disciples, must leave the world or at least lash our way through the world and whip the world into declaring open war on the name of the Lord Jesus Christ, his faith, and his church, then we shall leave this to the scoffers themselves. For thus we have not learned to know Christ, we have not thus been taught by him, our sole teacher, master, who by no means would ask his and our heavenly Father to take us out of the world, but who prayed that he would keep us from evil. Likewise, at the entry into Jerusalem neither the Lord nor his disciples forbade the throng to intone hosanna to the Son of David, or admonished them for the sake of honesty immediately to shout: Crucify, crucify him!

Nor, in our times and in our circles, then, is there the least temptation for servants of the Lord to be perturbed by the fact that the world seemingly goes after the Lord, for among us unbelief is quite openly admitted by the world, so that when it wishes to be called Christian it generally admits that it does not pretend to believe in Jesus Christ or to expect forgiveness of sins and blessedness in his name and for his sake, but that it is only a badge of honor which it demands the right to wear because it is neither Jewish or Turkish but strives to become virtuous, following Christ's admonition and example, considering him a teacher come from God.

The one thing in this matter that we in our times and in our circles as servants of the Lord ask of the world is that it permit us who believe in the Lord Jesus Christ, God the Father's only Son and as man conceived by the Holy Spirit, to keep for ourselves our baptism in the name of the Father, the Son, and the Holy Spirit, and likewise let us who believe in the real presence of Christ's body and blood in the Lord's Supper, keep our Holy Communion for ourselves. This we have asked and this we continue to ask of the world, all the while diligently informing the world that if it wishes to keep peace with the Lord Jesus Christ and to benefit materially by the presence of his spirit and gospel the best way is to leave his sacraments inviolate as well as undisputed, but for the rest, whenever it wishes, with us to admire and praise his matchless love of mankind, his blessed words and mighty deeds, his virtues which called us from darkness to his marvelous light!

Yes, my friends, as disciples of Christ such is our attitude toward that world which considers itself a part of Christendom and which calls itself Christian, without, however, wanting Christ to be lord or through our Lord Jesus Christ's faith, hope, and love wanting to seek righteousness, peace, and joy. And when scoffers shout that as long as we keep a truce with the world, and even let ourselves be sustained physically by the world while we preach the gospel of Christ, we ourselves are just as far as the world from our Lord Jesus Christ and from the Christianity of the New Testament which verily demands utter poverty, life-and-death struggle with the world, and hatred of our own lives and of those who in their desire to be true disciples of Christ take up their cross and follow him—then our answer is simply that these mockeries are as old in the world as the new covenant, and still older than what is called the New Testament, inasmuch as it was said of our Lord Jesus Christ himself: he is a glutton and a wine bibber. It was found that the very costly jar of pure nard ointment wasted on his body ought rather to have been sold for three hundred denarii and given to the poor; and found also that what the wealthy and worldly men Joseph of Arimathea and Nicodemus did to provide the crucified an expensive funeral constituted the suitable ending to the life of a genuine truth-witness among malefactors. All such scoffing is very old and it can get much older without causing a single one of the servants of our Lord Jesus Christ to commit suicide, to flee from his Lord and follow the world, or to sell him for thirty pieces of silver, for barrels of gold, or for all the kingdoms of the world with their splendors, and without our Lord Jesus Christ therefore rejecting a single one of his servants, young or old, turning his back on him in affluence or in need, by evil or good report, during days of truce or days of battle, in life or in death.

Just as certain, then, as the fact that the world never goes to the Lord, even though it appeared so at the entry into Jerusalem, just as certain is the fact that his disciples never go away from him no matter how far they lag behind in following him; for the Lord never leaves them, though it seemed so at his ascension and during the dispirited times his church recently lived through and was defiled by. He has placed his Spirit on us and laid his word on our lips and it shall not depart from our lips and the lips of our descendants forever. That his word to us is spirit and life shall not only the world realize more and more clearly, but his whole church shall feel it with ever increasing joy and fervor, with or without the will of the world. It shall sing its hosanna to the Son of David and praise the Spirit which issues from the Father and comes to all of us in the name of the Lord Jesus Christ with his righteousness, his peace, and his joy which lasts forevermore! Amen!

Good Friday
1855

Father of our Lord Jesus Christ, and our Father! Maker of heaven and earth! Thy Word to us through thy only Son is spirit and life, the Word of faith, hope, and love which must be heard, believed, and confessed, so that thy good works through thy Holy Spirit can be fulfilled among us until the day of our Lord Jesus Christ. Our Father, who art in heaven!

Christian friends! That tree of the cross which Simon of Cyrene carried for Christ, and on which the Lord bore our sins, has, no doubt, long since crumbled away; for since that was the fate of all the green trees on Mount Olive in Gethsemane and the cedars of Lebanon, how much more so with the dry, withered tree, hewn for pain and raised for derision of the Lord. Although we by no means participate in the ridicule of that someone who in times past with loving care dug deeply into the knoll of Golgotha in order to find possibly a splinter of the cross on which the Savior of the world suffered and died—yes, although we ask the learned scoffers why worshipers of Rome dig in the seven hills and in a thousand mounds, trying to find links of the chains with which Rome bound the world, it is still clear to us enlightened Christians that neither the tree of the cross, if we found it whole and complete, nor the robe of the Lord for which the Roman soldiers cast lots under the cross, nor anything else that had something to do with Christ in the days of his flesh are able to help us or have the least to do with our worship and adoration of the Crucified One. This adoration is to be worship solely in spirit and in truth, so that we must say with the apostle: though we had known Christ in the flesh, we still would not know him; for if anyone is in Christ he is a new creature, the old has passed away, behold, the new has come [2 Cor. 5:16-17].

104

As we come from the *tree of the cross* to the *sign of the cross,* it is already something different; for the sign of the cross is the same at all times and hovers on the boundary between the visible and the invisible, the physical and the spiritual; and we are all marked with this sign on our foreheads and on our breasts in holy baptism, so that there can be no possible thought or talk among Christians either of ridiculing the sign of the cross, regardless of how it has been and is abused, or avoiding or disdaining it.   Moreover, it is touching for all Christians to hear how in the days of the great crusades large parts of Christendom fought eagerly for the holy sepulcher and the Holy Land under the banner of the cross.   There were people, probably from the north, who arrived in a harbor in the south where no one understood their language but where they were recognized as Christians by placing their fingers in the shape of a cross.   Thus the sign of the cross is the only means by which a deaf-mute is able to indicate that he believes in Christ, and we can think of the cross as a deaf-mute who points to the One crucified for all of us for the sake of him to whom that cross refers.

Notwithstanding this, as enlightened Christians we cannot ever attribute either Christian worth or Christian power to the mere sign; for, like the water in baptism and the bread and wine in Communion, the sign of the cross is not Christian in itself but becomes so only when Christ's name is added; it becomes the sign of *Christ's cross* only when expressed emphatically as in baptism, so that we thereby reveal that we belong to the crucified Lord Jesus Christ.

Thus we come to the *word of the cross* which has been, and probably always will be, the object of the world's derision and indignation, even more so than the tree of the cross or the sign of the cross.   Here we all know that we stand on Christian ground, not only because the word of the cross contains the scriptural evidence that it is a folly only to those who are perishing, but to us who are being saved it is the power of God [1 Cor. 1:18], but because first and last, as human words and what they achieve constitute the humanity in us that lifts us above dumb creatures, just so the Word of God, and what it does, constitutes the divine, the Word of our Lord Jesus Christ and what it does, all that we can know and recognize as Christian in spirit and in truth.

But here we are confronted with a question of conscience as to whether or not this word of the cross lives among us as a Word of God and acts among us as a power from God.   Here it may seem as if we not only can but must answer No; for even in our so-called Lenten sermons very little is said about Christ's cross and almost nothing about his wounds by which we are healed; and our daily life hardly demonstrates that we take up the cross and follow the Crucified One, which surely, according to Scripture, should be proof that the word of the cross is God's power within us.   Although it is somewhat obscure when the apostle writes that through the cross the world is crucified to him and he to the world [Gal. 6:14], it is clear enough that the apostle thereby reveals how deep an imprint the word of Christ's cross had made on his heart, his whole life, and his total outlook on life in this world.

But, Christian friends, when we, as children of the light and the day, immediately admit, which is true, that the word of the cross still is not as close to our hearts as it is eloquent on our lips, or as deep and evident an influence in our lives in this world as Scripture reveals about the apostle Paul, whose heart and tongue and entire being became wholly new, we nevertheless boldly challenge the unreasonable and un-Christian allegation that we are not true Christians because we have not reached the Christian perfection which the apostle describes.   This is as if we would deny that our children were genuine human beings because they are as yet far from knowing, or in word and deed unable to express, their humanity as vigorously or as clearly as we are.   For to harbor the mistaken notion that the Christian's spiritual life is unlike his physical life, with its childhood and youth before it reaches manhood, is to reveal a fatal misconcept of Christian life and an ignorance of the Scriptures, which teach us that even God's only Son when be became incarnate matured through thirty years before he became the full-grown and perfect new man in whom God's Spirit could abide and of whom the Father testified: this is my beloved Son in whom I am well pleased. It can only be in our Lord's own footsteps that we can approach and reach him; for it cannot be wisdom but folly to imagine that we can achieve Christ's full stature without growing and advancing in years, wisdom, and grace before God and man, just as he did, or that one of us can begin where he finished, or that we can fully possess the word of the cross before we have learned to bear our cross as well as he bore his, knowing that the burden is light because he who bears all with his almighty Word is with us!

Therefore, Christian friends, we say in truth that when Christians speak overmuch of Christ's cross and when they suffer it as a heavy burden the word of the cross has become dead for them and verily dead in them. Then the word of the cross has become a letter of the law which kills, not an evangelical God-power in the Spirit which engenders life. But when we, though far from Christian perfection in this as in all matters, freely confess with the apostle, as in truth we can, that we will know of no other Christ, no other savior, or no other God's only son crucified [1 Cor. 2:1-2] than that Jesus Christ who was born of the Virgin Mary and crucified under Pontius Pilate, then the word of the cross is also living among us. If it has been dead it has risen again as he rose from death, and by the same power from God. Then, hereafter, it will also be manifest in the life and manner of the church that it is by the power of our Lord Jesus Christ's resurrection that we gradually reach his suffering community and fellowship. As it is in baptism, that God-man will be born who will rest by the Lord's bosom through Holy Communion and become like him who was crucified for us. Amen!

8th Sunday after Trinity
1855

Father of our Lord Jesus Christ and our heavenly Father! Creator of heaven and earth! Thy Word is truth, and through thy only-begotten Son it gives us spirit and life—that Word of faith and hope and love which must be heard, believed, and confessed, so that through the Holy Spirit thy good deed may be fulfilled among us until the day of our Lord Jesus Christ! Our Father, who art in heaven!

"Beware of false prophets, who come to you in sheep's clothing but inwardly are ravenous wolves" [Matt. 7:15].

We appointed pastors have often used this warning by our Lord Jesus Christ against false prophets when speaking of those who pointed toward another road to salvation than we do. No wonder, therefore, that the others, if they dare, use the same warning against us, for here also it is true that "the measure you give will be the measure you get" [Matt. 7:2], and since we first and last are called and appointed by the Lord himself to be preachers of his gospel we must also endure the slander of being called false prophets and wolves in sheep's clothing. Our Lord Jesus Christ has not only prepared us for this with the words "If they have called the master of the house Beelzebul, how much more will they malign those of his household" [Matt. 10:25], but he has also betimely comforted all of his disciples faced with buffeting by the world with the winsome words "Blessed are you when men revile you and persecute you and utter all kinds of evil against you falsely on my account. Rejoice and be glad, for your reward is great in heaven, for so men persecuted the prophets who were before you" [Matt. 5:11-12].

Yes, my friends, we who now are sent to preach the gospel in the name of our Lord Jesus Christ have less reason to whimper when we are labeled worse than blind guides, deliberate deceivers, false prophets, and ravenous wolves. It must be clear to us that the more freely we are contradicted, abused, and insulted, the more persuasive and credible our witness will be, because our situation comes to resemble that of the Lord and his apostles. The more vigorous spirit of truth will then witness through us to all who are of the truth that we speak only because we believe and that the road we point to is the narrow road which leads to the land of the living. We point to no other way than our Lord Jesus Christ who himself is the way, the truth, and the life.

And see this, my friends, while all the broad roads which are said to lead toward heaven lead only to hell, it is by no means all narrow roads that lead to heaven, but only the one very narrow way: Jesus Christ himself. This surely needs to be elucidated and emphasized also in our times, for while on the one hand some consider it sufficient to say, "Lord, Lord," to Jesus Christ, in spite of the Lord's emphatic words in today's gospel, others hold that to do the heavenly Father's will—without Jesus Christ—is to deny oneself and to conquer the world. The road and gate to heaven would undeniably be small and narrow enough; but that road would obviously be impassable for every one of us, just as it also and clearly is un-Christian according to the Lord's words, "I am the vine, you are the branches . . . apart from me you can do nothing" [John 15:5].

The truth is that since our Lord Jesus Christ himself is the way, the only living way, to the heavenly Father's house, then all the heaven-bound roads we ourselves can discover or prepare are misleading and dead-end roads, whether they are broad or narrow. On the other hand, it is not sufficient to say that we see the right road in Jesus Christ; we must also follow it if it is to lead us to the goal. Jesus Christ himself has explained the matter in the gospel of the day by saying: "Every one then who hears these words of mine and does them will be like a wise man who built his house upon the rock; and the rain fell, and the floods came, and the winds blew and beat upon that house, but it did not fall, because it had been founded on the rock. And every one who hears these words of mine and does not do them will be like a foolish man who built his house upon the sand; and the rain fell, and the floods came, and the winds blew and beat against that house, and it fell; and great was the fall of it" [Matt. 7:24-27].

Therefore it is not enough to assure salvation for us who preach the gospel that we proclaim the true evangel and, like John the Baptizer, point to Jesus Christ as the Lamb of God who takes away the sin of the world, that we give witness to him as the only vine on earth that bears good fruit toward eternal life, and that we give witness to him as the way, the truth, and the life, without whom no one comes to the Father. All this is not enough to assure our salvation, for the Lord himself witnesses that many will approach him on the last day and say, " 'Lord, Lord, did we not prophesy in your name, and cast out demons in your name, and do many mighty works in your name?' And then will I declare to them, 'I never knew you; depart from me, you evildoers' " [Matt. 7:22-23]. Although it is not sufficient for salvation to preach Jesus Christ and him alone as the way, the truth, and the life, it is sufficient for those who hear these words and act on them, so that deeds follow words and Jesus Christ really becomes their heavenly way, truth, and life. Then they will know that we were not false but true prophets, since our prediction was fulfilled: that Jesus Christ whom we proclaimed proved for them to be the sound tree which bore not evil but good and eternal fruit.

Yes, my friends, the true Christian life, the life of our Lord Jesus Christ in his believing congregation and the churches' life through him, is the fruit by which we are to be known as true prophets according to the Lord's words, "Are grapes gathered from thorns, or figs from thistles?" [Matt. 7:16]. But this Christian life, this life in the Lord, is by no means what the false prophets proclaim, a life of constant sorrow and anguish, pain and plague, for such was not the life which our Lord Jesus Christ himself lived on earth; and we shall become as he was in this world. Who can doubt that the life of our Lord Jesus Christ, despite his worldly lowliness, poverty, adversity, and temptation and, when his hour of suffering came, even pain and death, still was in its totality the most joyful, the most blissful human life that has been and ever can be lived in this world. Hence the apostle writes, "sorrowful, yet always rejoicing!" [2 Cor. 6:10].

Therefore, my friends, let this stand: the Lord Jesus Christ whom

we confess in baptism with the word of faith from his own lips, who
regenerates us in baptism with his heavenly Father's Word and
Spirit, and who nourishes us in the Eucharist, he is the way, the
truth, and the life. With him, but not without him, all believing
hearts and truth-loving souls come to heaven. This is our prophecy,
our prediction, in the name of our Lord Jesus and his Spirit which
issues from the Father. The louder and the more acridly the world
labels us false prophets and ravenous wolves in sheeps' clothing, the
deeper will be the impression of our prediction upon the friends of
truth, and the more clearly will they see that we are true prophets,
not like the wolves but faithful shepherds who gather the flock and
lead it to streams of living waters, sheltering and protecting it.
Therefore we rejoice and confidently address the Lord's church with
the words of the apostle, "Rejoice in the Lord always; again I will
say, Rejoice. . . .The Lord is at hand" [Phil. 4:4-5]. The Lord be
with you. Amen!

4th Sunday after Easter

1855

Father of our Lord Jesus Christ, and our Father! Maker of heaven and earth! The Word to us through thy only son is spirit and life, the Word of faith, hope, and love which must be heard, believed, and confessed, so that thy good works through thy Holy Spirit can be fulfilled among us until the day of our Lord Jesus Christ. Our Father, who art in heaven!

"I have yet many things to say to you, but you cannot bear them now. When the Spirit of truth comes, he will guide you into all the truth; for he will not speak on his own authority, but whatever he hears he will speak, and he will declare to you the things that are to come. He will glorify me, for he will take what is mine and declare it to you. All that the Father has is mine; therefore I said that he will take what is mine and declare it to you" [John 16:12-15].

These prophetic words from the Lord's farewell address to his disciples prior to his suffering and death no doubt came true for his apostles and for the whole Christian church, which followed the Lord's resurrection and ascension. Then the Spirit of truth which proceeds from the Father and glorifies the Son came to rest on them and equipped them with both power and wisdom from on high, so that they were able to acquire and to speak the whole truth in Jesus Christ our Lord.

But just as the Lord himself says that his word concerning eternal life shall never perish, so his prophecy concerning the condition and the future of his church is fulfilled only when the church reaches its goal. This goal is salvation, when we shall clearly see, face to face, the whole divine truth and clearly perceive what we have believed, hoped, and loved through the Word of God but have seen only dimly as in a mirror.

112

Therefore, Christian friends, it is natural now, as it has always been and always will be, for elders of the church to take leave of the children in Christ in the same manner that the Lord took leave of his first disciples. For we, too, have much to say to the children in the name of the Lord Jesus Christ which they cannot yet bear, but toward which the Spirit of truth will guide them when they permit him. For, as written, though gifts of grace differ, the Spirit is the same, as is the goal: salvation and comprehension of truth by the grace of the Holy Spirit for all of us who believe in the name of the only-begotten Son.

But I must repeat today, Christian friends, what I often have said and witnessed in my congregation, that the Lord's prophetic words in the gospel today concerning the outpouring of the Holy Spirit on his church toward affirmation of the true faith and toward growing enlightenment and eternal consolation must be closer to the hearts and more frequent on the lips of those of us who allow ourselves to be driven by the Lord's Spirit than has been the case since the days of the apostles. In the Lord's church, much more so than outside it, there is apparently a transition period, the biggest, the most hazardous but, God be praised, also the most hopeful and most consolatory transition period the church has experienced and can experience before the final transition period from corruption to incorruption, from mortality to immortality, from temporality to eternity, from suffering to salvation.

For there is verily now a great transition period from darkness to light and from death to life in a spiritual sense, unlike anything else since the time of the forty days, when the resurrected Lord appeared and disappeared as the lightning flashes from east to west, spoke to his disciples about the kingdom of God so that their hearts burned within them, although their eyes were veiled so that they failed to recognize him, and breathed into them his peace, although their hearts were still reluctant to believe all that the prophets had said concerning Christ's suffering and entrance to his glory.

Yes, Christian friends, since the days of my youth when the Lord first shed light upon my soul as fires are lit upon the eternal hills, I perceived clearly what the Lord says: the flesh is of no avail; it is the Spirit that gives life—perceived how far it reaches, so that even the incarnation of the Only-Begotten would be of no avail had he not sent us that Spirit which enlivens souls and hearts by his faith, hope, and love. Thus it was to the advantage for his first as well as for his last disciples that he went away, since he himself bears witness that had he not returned to his father, the divine Companion and eternal Comforter would not have come in his name, inscribing his name in our hearts and our names in the book of life, not with ink but with the Spirit of the living God.

From that day to this day with my gray hair, it has been clear as day to me that this is a transition period for the whole church as well as for me, from darkness to light and from death to life, concerning what belongs to the kingdom of God. This alone comforted me when I felt that I had much to say, both to you and to old fellow Christians, which they could not yet bear. They did not know what I meant when I emphasized the word of the apostle that not our own life but only the life of him who died and rose for us is the real and true Christian life, and that what we ourselves may think of in the service of the new covenant does not lead to salvation. All our competence in the service of the new covenant and the new life is from God who gives us his holy and quickening Spirit, so that we are preachers of the true gospel only when we ourselves do not speak, but the Father's Spirit is speaking through us, using us not as inanimate objects but as willing and joyful instruments!

Yes, this has been and still remains my comfort that for the whole church of the Lord this is a great transition period, from darkness to light and from death to life, and then from clarity to clarity in all spiritual matters for groups with faith, hope, and love, so that, even if it does not happen before I pass away and go home to him who sent me, to that Lord whose redeemed slave and servant I am, what has happened to me shall surely happen to the whole church of the Lord. The church shall lift up its eyes to the hills, to the eternal heights from whence help shall come, shall perceive light in the light of the Lord, and shall receive the fullness of the spiritual riches, which we have in earthen vessels and which, according to Scripture, we bear in earthen vessels to show that the transcendent power belongs to God and not to us.

And look, my friends, this happens and happens only when the

Spirit of the Son, our Lord Jesus Christ, which proceeds from the Father, the Spirit of eternal truth and eternal love, the deity's own life-power, again is strongly felt in the church and is received with praise as the one that comes in the name of our Lord Jesus Christ. He is distinguishable from all false spirits by confession of the incarnate Jesus Christ and on the word of the Lord, that he will not speak on his own authority, although he sees all things, also the depths of God, but speaks only that which he hears. He speaks the same words the Lord in the days of his flesh had laid upon the lips of his apostles and through them the whole church, speaks only words of eternal life. He calls forth its light like unto the light of God's face and reflects the glory of God, so that the church feels the real presence of our Lord Jesus Christ, although the world does not see him. He reveals himself spiritually for all those who hold fast his word with proof as plain as when he revealed himself to his friends after the resurrection and spoke to them about matters that pertain to the kingdom of God. He tells us that he can and will dwell in his church and walk in it as the only-begotten Son from eternity in all the regenerated sons and daughters whom the heavenly Father and the Son embrace, sharing his glory.

Then, and only then, God's kingdom comes to us, not so that one can point to it and say: look here or look there, as one points to the great nations, but in such a way that the whole church lives in it, saying and singing: Now we know that God's kingdom is truly righteousness, peace, and joy in the Holy Spirit. It comes as the Spirit proclaims in deeds and truths what is to come through that which is now worked and created in us. Then we cannot for a moment doubt that what now lives in us, a real and joyful power, though concealed, shall be revealed when he who is our life comes again even as he ascended. Thus it follows that the sufferings of this present time are not worth comparing with the glory that is to be revealed to us, just as surely as this glory has descended and rests upon us.

Therefore, Christian friends, we will not be fearful or despondent in the great transition period from darkness to light, from death to life, and from clarity to clarity, for it holds true throughout the lives of all God's children in this world, and not only during their last days, that they shall not fear evil as they walk through the valley of the shadow of death. We who walked in darkness have seen a great light, and he who is the light of the world is with us so that we perceive that it is sin not to believe in him who is truth, light, and life. It was well that he left us physically for a little while in order that we might have him with us spiritually throughout eternity. And the prince of this world is judged as the father of lies whose wisdom is darkness, whose achievement is death, and who scorns him who dwells within us: the Spirit of truth and light who quickens us eternally! Amen!

HYMNS AND POETRY

Grundtvig's Hymns and Poetry

by JOHANNES KNUDSEN

One's first reaction to Grundtvig's treasure of hymns is to be over-whelmed. The beholder is awed by its sheer volume. Numbers are difficult to give, for the collections of hymns are interspersed by biblical songs and other poetry. Grundtvig wrote night and day through an incredibly long career, and the hymns alone are counted in numbers of four figures. Not all of these have equal value, but it is an impressive fact that in the most recent hymnal of the Church of Denmark, published in 1955, the number of hymns attributed to Grundtvig was increased to 272, out of a total of 754 in the hymnal.

The inspiration for these hymns came from many sources, but by far the greatest number take their theme and content from the Bible. The church with its proclamation and its worship furnish the subject for a great many, and the Christian life is examined, exalted, and given voice in many others. The great festivals of the church year are celebrated, with perhaps Pentecost and the work of the Holy Spirit getting the most attention. Grundtvig also re-created many hymns from varying sources, from older Danish hymnody, from German and English hymns, from ancient Latin and Greek worship hymns, etc.

While Grundtvig's prose is verbose and repetitious, as anyone who has gone through the documents up to this point will know, his poetry is precise and filled with imagery, much of it nature illustrations. His profoundest insights are crystallized into sparkling gems by the pressure of the bound form. In contrast to ideas of freedom of expression that prevail today, where vague expansiveness is the offspring of freedom, older generations of poets were liberated to precise and poetic expressions of genius and inspiration by the free-dom of doing what has to be done. The bound metricity of verse

119

and the ascending lilt of music has given the spirit of man innumerable opportunities of creativeness and clarification, and Grundtvig has seized upon a great number of these.

His song is a song of the church, its proclamation and its life of fellowship, and his song has become an integral part of the worship of his countrymen. Where other peoples have to rely on the monotonous repetition of ancient formulas in the requirements of worship, the Danish congregation participates with fervor in the liturgy through multitudinous choices of Grundtvig's hymns, which express in varying and lively ways what the barnacled rituals can say only in drab repetition.

The bind of form, which can be liberating for the genius of the hymn-writer, works in reverse for the translator. He feels bound by the meter and the melody and especially by the rhyme of the original. The translator has three restricting guidelines; he must transfer the *content* of the original in a felicitous manner, and he must not violate the *form* and the *imagery* of its verse. Very often, therefore, he is caught up in a dilemma where he is tempted to sacrifice something of the content by being overly loyal to either form or imagery. Many examples can be given of the distortion or alteration of hymns by overzealous translators fascinated by their own invention of rhyme. Well-known Grundtvig translations illustrate this. An overconcern for the rhythm and rhyme of the first lines had led the translator to say "Built on a rock the church doth stand," when the original says "Throughout the years the church does stand," literally "The church is an ancient house." Misunderstandings of words and images, and especially of subtleties, can alter hymns. The last verse of "O Day Full of Grace" begins with a Danish word that means either "thus" or "then." It is obvious that Grundtvig meant "thus," thereby describing the total Christian life, on earth and in heaven. The translator, however, says "then," when he translates, "With joy we depart for our fatherland." Worst of all wrongs is, of course, the deliberate alteration in translation. Many of Grundtvig's hymns have been changed to pietistic expressions of the Christian life that alter the message.

It is therefore difficult to present competent, poetic, felicitous, and singable translation. When we do present a number of these it is because Grundtvig's thought must be represented also by his hymns and because prose paraphrases are so dreadfully uninviting. The number of translations offered here is limited because some of the translations of great hymns cannot measure up to the criteria of being competent, poetic, and felicitous to the original. In addition to the translation of hymns, we are including songs or poems that are relevant to his educational philosophy. One important poem, concerning the nature of humanity and Christianity, is offered in paraphrase. It is overly hard to translate it poetically and it has not been used as a song.

*   *   *

O day full of grace, which we behold,
Now gently to view ascending,
Thou over the earth thy reign unfold,
Good cheer to all mortals lending,
That children of light of every clime
May prove that the night is ending!

How blest was that gracious morning hour,
When God in our flesh was given;
Then flushed the dawn with light and power,
That spread through the darkened heaven;
Then rose o'er the world that sun divine,
Which gloom from our hearts has driven.

Yea, were every tree endowed with speech,
And every leaflet singing,
They never with praise his worth could reach,
Though earth with their praise were ringing,
Who fully could praise the light of life,
Who light to our souls is bringing.

As birds in the morning sing God's praise,
His fatherly love we cherish,
For giving to us this day of grace,

For life that shall never perish,
His church he has kept these thousand years,
And hungering soul did nourish.

We journey unto our fatherland,
Where day is not frail nor fleeting.
We vision a mansion, fair and grand,
Where joyously friends are meeting.
This life we shall share eternally,
Its dawn we are always greeting.

Translated by Carl Døving
Last verse translated by Johannes Knudsen

*   *   *

Throughout the years the church does stand,
Even when steeples are falling;
Crumbled have spires in every land,
Bells still are chiming and calling;
Calling the young and old to rest,
But above all the soul distrest,
Longing for rest everlasting.

Surely in temples made with hands,
God, the most high, is not dwelling,
High above earth his temple stands,
All earthly temples excelling;
Yet, he whom heavens cannot contain
Chose to abide on earth with men,
Built in our bodies his temple.

We are God's house of living stones,
Builded for his habitation;
He through baptismal grace us owns,
Heirs of his wondrous salvation;
Were we but two his name to tell,
Yet, he would deign with us to dwell,
With all his grace and his favor.

Still we our earthly temples rear,
That we may herald his praises;
They are the homes where he draws near
And little children embraces;
Beautiful things in them are said,
God there with us his covenant made,
Making us heirs of his kingdom.

Here stands the font before our eyes,
Telling how God did receive us;
The altar recalls Christ's sacrifice
And what his table does give us;
Here sounds the Word that does proclaim
Christ yesterday, today the same,
Yea, and for aye our redeemer.

Grant then, O God, where'er men roam,
That when the church bells are ringing,
Many in Jesus' faith may come
Where he his message is bringing;
I know mine own, mine own know me,
Ye, not the world, my face shall see;
My peace I leave with you, Amen!

Translated by Carl Døving
First line altered

*　　*　　*

God's people receive
Through Christ what the world cannot know nor believe.
This while we are here we but dimly can know,
Though feeling within us its heavenly glow.
The Lord says: My kingdom, the home of my love,
Is here and above.

How blessed to be
Where death has no sting, where from sin we are free,
Where all that decayed in new glory shall bloom,

Where all that was ruined shall rise from the tomb,
Where love grows in light as a summer day fair
With flower-crowned hair.

How blessed the land,
Where time is not measured by tears or with sand,
Where fades not the flower, the bird never dies,
Where joys are not bubbles that break as they rise,
Where life does not crown us with white for the gloom
Of death and the tomb.

O land of our king,
Where harvest embraces the flowery spring,
Where all things worth having forever remain,
Where nothing we miss but our sorrow and pain,
This kingdom we hail, as we herald abroad
The promise of God.

                              Translated by Søren D. Rodholm
                    Revised and rearranged by Johannes Knudsen

*   *   *

Fair beyond telling
Lord, is your dwelling,
Wondrous to see!
My heart is yearning,
Eagerly turning
Ever to be
Safe in your temple to worship, O Lord,
With you communing in deepest accord.

With your compassion,
Lord of salvation,
Naught can compare.
Even the sparrow,
Safe from the arrow,
Rests in your care;
And as you shield the frail bird in its nest,
So let my heart in your temple find rest.

Years full of splendors,
Which to offenders
Earth may afford,
Never can measure
One day of pleasure
Found with you, Lord,
When on the wings of your quickening word
Souls beyond galaxies upward have soared.

Rich in your blessing,
Upward progressing
Are now your friends,
Strengthened in spirit
Each by your merit
Upward ascends
Till, when at home in that city of gold,
All shall in wonder your presence behold.

Translated by Jens C. Aaberg
Revised by Johannes Knudsen

*   *   *

Most wondrous is of all on earth
The kingdom Jesus founded,
Its glory, peace, and precious worth
No tongue has ever sounded.

As breath of wind invisible,
Its signs are yet revealed;
A city set upon a hill
From men is not concealed.

Its secret—God's almighty Word
Which heav'n and earth created,
The valleys when His voice they heard
Were filled, the floods abated.

The tempter by his evil power
The kingdom is distressing,

God crowns in His appointed hour
With joy and fruitful blessing.

It shines like golden harvest ear,
Or leaves of beechwood springing;
Like waves in sun it will appear
While birds in flight are singing.

Its glorious king is He who died
Upon the cross to save us,
New joy unto the world to bring
His very life He gave us.

And when He comes again to reign
The strife will have an ending;
What yet to faith was not made plain
The bless'd are comprehending.

Then comes the year of Jubilee,
Fulfilled the age-long story;
The heavenly reign shall all men see
Of justice, peace, and glory.

Translated by Jean Fraser

*   *   *

In our midst God's kingdom liveth
Through his spirit, by His word;
In His church new life He giveth,
Spreading there His festal board.

Though this kingdom may be hidden,
—Lo, not here, and lo, not there—
We as guests are sought and bidden,
Peace and joy are everywhere.

When in faith this life possessing,
Through His word, in Jesus' name,

All His kingdom's richest blessing
We, His children, gladly claim.

God's own justice, born in heaven,
By His grace descends to earth,
And His peace, in myst'ry given,
Proves within our hearts its worth.

When His joy—pure, rich, incessant—
By the spirit is proclaimed,
God's own realm is truly present,
We, His children, rightly named.

In the God-appointed hour,
At His pleasure, by His grace,
This, our life, shall grow and flower,
Bearing fruit in every place.

For the fullness of creation,
Faith and hope and love, these three,
Will be brought to consummation
By God's grace eternally.

Then the kingdom's fullest measure,
By His grace who gave us birth,
We shall share and fully treasure,
As in heaven so on earth.

                        Translated by Johannes Knudsen

                    *   *   *

The sun now shines in all its splendor,
The light of life with mercy tender;
Now bright Whitsunday lilies grow
And summer sparkles high and low;
Sweet voices sing of harvest gold
In Jesus' name a thousandfold.

The peaceful nightingales are filling
The summer night with music thrilling,
So all that to the Lord belong
May sleep in peace and wake with song,
May dream anew of paradise
And with God's praise at daylight rise.

It breathes from heaven on the flowers,
It whispers home-like in the bowers,
A balmy breeze comes to our shore
From paradise, now closed no more,
And gently purls the brooklet sweet
Of life's clear water at our feet.

Thus works the Spirit, still descending,
And tongues of fire to mortals lending,
That broken hearts may yet be healed
And truth may be in love revealed
In him who came from yonder land
And has returned to God's right hand.

Awake, ye voices, deep and ringing,
And anthems to the Lord be singing;
Your beauties lend, ye varied tongues,
To praise his name in joyful songs,
And ye, his church, with one accord,
Arise and glorify the Lord.

Translated by Søren D. Rodholm

*   *   *

Spirit of God, sent from heaven abroad,
Witnessing, judging, explaining,
Speak to mankind in its self-centered mind,
Comforting, guiding, sustaining,
Bring us your gospel, beside us stand,
Night with its darkness is near at hand.

Tongues as of fire, kindling words that inspire,
Grant to the ones you are sending
Filled with your lore as apostles of yore,
On one great quest never ending,
Until the very last heart is stirred,
Every last soul has been brought your word.

Growth springs alive as good tidings arrive,
Harvest will come on the morrow,
Strength will replace any weakness we face,
Comfort and hope for all sorrow,
Gently the gospel fulfills its task,
Mercy is given to all who ask.

Brighten our day as a morning in May,
Springtime erupting in beauty,
Bless us with joy as our gifts we employ,
Grace casting light over duty;
Anthems profoundly at eventide
Mellow the heart that was filled with pride.

As we baptize heaven's glory we prize.
Nations reborn by its power;
Witness we give that in grace we shall live,
God-given beauty shall flower.
Tree of our life root in Calvary's rood,
All men bear witness that God is good!

                              Translated by Johannes Knudsen

                    *   *   *

O Holy Spirit, come, we pray,
And give us light to guide us on our way,
And in times most trying
Help us not to waver;
Keep us from denying
Jesus Christ, our Savior.
Hear our prayer, O Lord!

O Holy Spirit, blessed light,
Come, teach us Jesus Christ to know aright,
That to him we render
Praise and adoration
For his mercy tender,
For his free salvation.
Hear our prayer, O Lord!

O Holy Spirit, come to move
Our hearts in Christian fellowship and love,
That, in peace and gladness,
Brother walk with brother,
Spreading joy for sadness,
Loving one another.
Hear our prayer, O Lord!

O Holy Spirit, cheer our hearts,
As mother comfort to her child imparts,
Till our sorrows vanish
Through your love eternal,
Till our cares we banish
Through your blessings vernal.
Hear our prayer, O Lord!

O Holy Spirit, come to prove
That we possess our heavenly Father's love
Then our faith grows stronger,
Then our hopes we treasure;
Death shall rule no longer,
Heaven holds our pleasure.
Hear our prayer, O Lord!

Martin Luther
Adapted to the Danish by N. F. S. Grundtvig
Translated by P. C. Paulsen

*   *   *

Blossom shall the wilderness
Like a rose-filled bower,

Joy shall reign and happiness,
Desert lands shall flower.
Glory comes to Lebanon,
Carmel's height has splendor won,
Roses bloom in Sharon.

Sight is given to the blind
And their eyes shall glisten;
Every mute his voice shall find,
All the deaf shall listen;
Like the hart the lame shall leap,
Zion nevermore shall weep,
Peace shall reign forever.

Thus Isaiah prophesied
In the days of sadness,
Ages passed, then far and wide
Spread the news of gladness:
Christ is here, with us he stands,
Changing with his loving hands
Desert wastes to Eden.

Hail our king at God's right hand,
Jesus and his spirit!
Lead us to the promised land
We by faith inherit!
And though death be drawing near,
Words of life the deaf shall hear,
Mutes shall sing his praises.

                        Translated by Søren D. Rodholm
                  First verse revised by Johannes Knudsen

                    *   *   *

Holy Spirit, still our sorrow,
In our hearts your light reveal,
Turn our darkness into morrow
And the fount of life unseal;

Give us comfort, strength, and breath,
Light in darkness, life in death.

God's eternal might and glory
Lie revealed before your sight,
And salvation's wondrous story
You alone can bring to light
When to us from heaven above
You descended with God's love.

Maker of the new creation,
Prove in us what you can do,
Save us from the foe's temptation,
Through God's Word our faith renew,
Build your temple in our breast,
Fill your house with peace and rest.

Translated by Jens C. Aaberg

*   *   *

Grant me, God, the gift of singing,
That in anthems loud and ringing
I may shout your praise!
Help me share the joy and pleasure
To proclaim in richest measure
All your gracious ways!

Heav'n itself proclaims your glory,
Thus we start each morning's story
Singing to your name;
And when evening bells are tolling
Anthems loudly keep on rolling,
Chanting e'er the same.

Your creation's name is wonder,
Depths of wisdom we can ponder
Yet can never plumb.
Of your life's unequaled splendor

Praise deserving none can render,
Even bards are dumb.

Human life is frail and faulty,
Human tears are bitter, salty,
Like the grass we die.
Even heav'ns shall swell and perish,
But in all things we can cherish
Life with you on high.

From your kingdom's life eternal
We are moved to pastures vernal,
Our God-given place.
All creation's harvest sharing,
Finest fruit we shall be bearing
By God's love and grace.

Translated by Johannes Knudsen

*   *   *

Dare we yet recall the tender,
Hopeful dreams of years gone by?
Though the world its judgment render,
Can for Zion still we cry?
Can we now, our harps attuning,
Sing a song of ancient days,
Anthems shouting, carols crooning,
Chant, Jerusalem, your praise?

Come, assemble by the mountain,
Zion's daughters, young and old!
They who conquered field and fountain
Zion's hill have not controlled.
Ruined all, by foe's commanding,
We have yet the cornerstone;
All the blows of arms withstanding,
It is firm and it alone.

Ours is not a temple, rearing
Tower and steeple to the sky;
Modest homes are now appearing,
Fruits of what we seek and try.
Yet when we in faith have striven
In the shadow of God's wings,
With a true foundation given,
We can build for better things.

Worldly greats, our efforts scorning,
May reject our humble homes,
Yet the glow of Easter morning
To the faithful richly comes.
In the lap of common people
Jesus laid his infant head,
Asking neither tower nor steeple,
Now he breaks with us his bread.

Great cathedrals tell their story,
Oft of falling arch or dome,
But the glow of heaven's glory
Lingers in our cottage home.
All the riches we can gather
Cannot match the love of God;
Through his Son, our loving Father,
Truly blessed our home, our sod.

                              Translated by Johannes Knudsen

                    *   *   *

Zechariah 4

As temple walls anew were rising,
God's people heard the prophet's voice;
Though days of small things now despising,
You faithful ones shall yet rejoice!
With Solomon do not compare,
But build your temple good and fair!

Be not dismayed when days are meager,
When greatness fades in gloom away,
When friends are mute and foes are eager,
And toil is endless through the day,
My spirit e'er will be with you,
In quiet tell you what to do.

Thus speaks our Lord in times most trying,
As we our battered church rebuild,
When foes their curses loud are crying
And friendly voices oft are stilled;
Do not despise the meager days,
But fill your church with songs of praise!

The threatening peaks that tower o'er us
Will never vanish, sight unseen,
But as the Spirit goes before us,
Shall level out to pastures green.
Nor might, nor power can afford,
But by my spirit, says the Lord.

Be not dismayed when walls do crumble,
We shall be given stones to build.
Be not dismayed though feet may stumble,
With strength from God we shall be filled.
The plummet is not man's alone,
We build on God's own cornerstone.

Do not despise the days so meager,
When hands are feeble, voices low!
For every small-time task be eager,
And watch how temple walls shall grow!
For God will bless us as we build,
His house shall be with glory filled.

Translated by Johannes Knudsen

*   *   *

God's little child, what troubles thee?
Children may to their father flee,
He will uphold them by his hand;
None can his might and grace withstand.
The Lord be praised!

Raiment and food and counsel tried
God for his children will provide;
They shall not starve, nor homeless roam,
Children may claim their father's home.
The Lord be praised!

Singing, the birds t'ward heaven soar,
Neither they reap nor lay in store,
Yet, where the hoarder dies from need,
Gathers the little bird a seed.
The Lord be praised!

Clad are the flowers in raiment fair,
Fairest to see on deserts bare,
Neither they spin, nor weave, nor sow,
Glory like theirs no king can show.
The Lord be praised!

Flowers that bloom at break of dawn,
Wither and die when day is gone,
How can they with the child compare
That shall his father's glory share.
The Lord be praised!

God's little child, do then fore'er
Cast on the Lord thy every care,
Trust in his love, his grace and might,
Then shall his peace thy soul delight.
The Lord be praised!

Raiment and food, thy daily bread,
He will provide as he has said,

And when his sun for thee goes down,
He will thy soul with glory crown.
The Lord be praised!

Translated by Jens C. Aaberg

*   *   *

God's angels of joy, we welcome you,
Your heavenly voices ringing,
You come to our world each year anew,
Of Christmas glory singing,
In soul-weary times a message true
Of peace, goodwill us bringing.

We welcome your song where'er you go,
On fields, in forest clearing,
On roadsides and streets now white with snow,
In church and home appearing,
Rekindle in us the heavenly glow,
Your great glad tidings hearing.

Come, sing for the children first of all,
In homes where lights are shining,
In cold-water flat and darkened hall,
With ne'er a silver lining.
Come, sing of a distant cattle stall,
A babe on straw reclining.

The children may dream of Bethlehem,
A child, a lowly manger,
A dream world, so strange to us and them,
Than fairies even stranger.
Come, enter their lives, make Jesse's stem
Their hope in lives of danger.

Then let them awaken Christmas Day
All filled with joy and gladness,
With tokens of gifts, with song and play,
Light up each home of sadness.

Make kindness and hope the shining ray
In world decay and madness.

Come, angels of God, to us descend,
Proclaim the life God gave us!
New vision and strength to mankind lend
Against what would enslave us!
God's love to all states of man extend!
His kingdom come to save us!

Translated and adapted by Johannes Knudsen

*   *   *

The last farewell to life on earth,
Its beauty and created worth,
Oft to despair has driven.
No one can ever be prepared,
Had not the Lord our life-lot shared,
His word of promise given.

My Jesus, Lord and brother true,
You shared the sting of death, and you
Have hell's dominion shaken.
Our true condition you have known,
Our deep despair was once your own,
By God you felt forsaken.

When you return, as we confess,
In final glory to suppress
All Satan's domination,
Be this at dawn, be this at night,
Your faithful ones will bless the sight,
The final consummation.

But should I die before you come,
Be at my bedside, in my home,
Mid death's grim, sordid story.
Let shine your light so I forget

The darkness of the tomb, and yet
See visions of your glory.

Come in the late, last watch at night,
Come as a loved one, known by sight,
To sit and talk beside me,
To speak to me as friend to friend
Of hope that we shall meet again,
To comfort and to guide me.

O, let me in my final hour
Take part in resurrection's power
To live in heaven yonder!
God, let me in your kingdom share,
Grant me the place that you prepare
In your eternal wonder.

Translated by Johannes Knudsen

*   *   *

Cradling children in his arm,
Jesus gave his blessing.
To our babes a welcome warm
He is yet addressing.
Take them, Lord, give life anew
In the living waters!
Keep them always near to you
As your sons and daughters!

Translated by Johannes Knudsen

*   *   *

God's word is our great heritage,
Our promise of salvation,
Proclaimed abroad from age to age
In every land and nation,
It is our living breath,
Our hope in face of death.
Whatever may befall,

Lord, grant your word may call
Each coming generation.

Translated by Johannes Knudsen

*   *   *

God's blessing falling on the earth
Is our great heritage at birth.
The blessing from the heavenly Lord
Is wine upon his festal board.

The blessing was to men proclaimed
When as God's people they were named,
But only when the "Word" was sown,
The covenant was truly known.

The blessing now, as dew and rain,
Descends on every hill and plain,
To all believers on God's earth
Baptismal grace gives second birth.

God's blessing, bountiful and true,
Will at the font our life renew,
And at the table we can share
A life with God beyond compare.

In hymns of gratitude and praise
God's people thankful voices raise.
God's blessing then, for one and all,
From open skies will on us fall.

Translated by Johannes Knudsen

*   *   *

Man first and then Christian
This is the order of life;
Even if we are called sheep we must not think
Of adding animals to the flock [of God]!
Even the Almighty cannot remake

Devils into Christians;
Therefore, do not throw pearls to swine.

The Baptizer was the greatest man
Among all the peers of David,
But greater yet than he
Is the smallest in the kingdom of God:
I.e., everyone who believes and is baptized,
Who is given the swaddling clothes of Christ,
In other words, every Christian.

Man first and then Christian,
This is a main article,
Christianity is given free,
It is purely our good fortune,
But a good fortune which only comes to him
Who already is a friend of God
By being of the noble tribe [or body] of truth.

Therefore every man on this earth
Must strive to be a true person,
To open his ears for the word of truth,
And to give God glory!
As Christianity then is the truth,
Even if he is not a Christian today,
He will be one tomorrow.

                    Prose translation by Johannes Knudsen

                    *   *   *

A plain and active joyful life on earth,
A treasure ne'er for power or gold to barter,
A guided life, the nobleness of birth
And equal dignity each human's charter,
A life created, tuned to the above,
Alert to man's God-granted gift for living,
Profoundly mindful of the need for love
Which God, the Father's, grace alone is giving.

A life like this I seek for all mankind.
I plan and work a fruitful growth preparing,
And when the seeking wearies out the mind,
The Lord's own pray-er gives me strength and daring.
The comfort of the spirit comes to me
That God has blessed our human, frail endeavor,
That in his hand alone our soul is free
And growth will come in nature's way forever.

A life created, tuned to that above!
A plant is rooted, fed by sun and showers,
The growth which reaps the care of nurture's love
Will find its harvest as a seed from flowers.
And though our day of years be short or long,
Creative growth we may to all be giving.
Our faithful efforts all to God belong,
And sunset glory crowns the gift of living.

                    Translated by Johannes Knudsen

                *   *   *

Relentlessly the human story
Moves like a river to the sea.
Our day of days, its growth and glory,
Can not prevail eternally.
But humankind does yet survive,
God's given image is alive.

For every fray that death is winning,
As worn-out warriors rest their sword,
God grants a new and fresh beginning
To man created by his Word,
And we retain, as ages move,
The memory of God's great love.

With hope we face the task of living,
The gift, the promise of our life,
Our constant effort ever giving

Against the foe's relentless strife.
Death's claim and power we defy,
God's saving grace gives victory.

Translated by Johannes Knudsen

*　　*　　*

In warmth of sunlight the plants unfold,
And true enlightenment fosters growing;
Of greater value than precious gold
'Tis God and self to be truly knowing.
　　Though night may frighten,
　　The sunbeams brighten,
　　They warm and lighten
　　The blessing clear.

The sun shines brightly as spring breaks through,
It guides the growth to its summer pleasure.
So true enlightenment brings to view
The growing values our hearts may treasure.
　　Though night may frighten,
　　The sunbeams brighten,
　　They warm and lighten
　　The heart's desire.

As growth takes over in plots and fields,
When days are warm and the nights are living,
True life-enlightenment grants its yield,
Its youthful blessing to hearts now giving.
　　Though night may frighten,
　　The sunbeams brighten,
　　They warm and lighten
　　The fertile soil.

As birds are filling the air with song,
When early growth has the fields in clover,
Our mother tongue as an anthem strong
Shall fill the youth as the light takes over.

Though night may frighten,
The sunbeams brighten,
They warm and lighten
The song so clear.

The Lord spoke out and the light was born;
As truth is loved and the light is savored,
So through His blessing who laughs at scorn,
Our efforts shall by His grace be favored.
Though night may frighten,
The sunbeams brighten,
They warm and lighten,
Our teaching task.

Translated by Johannes Knudsen

EDUCATIONAL WRITINGS

Grundtvig's Educational Writings

by JOHANNES KNUDSEN

Grundtvig received an academic education in the Latin preparatory schools and in the University of Copenhagen, graduating with a degree in theology in 1801. He was well-founded in the propaedeutics of his time, including the classical languages, and he absorbed the philosophical methods of the eighteenth-century Enlightenment. Throughout his life the logic of this philosophy remained as an element in his thinking, particularly the Principle of Contradiction. He disliked the schools heartily, however, claiming that their rote learning and their stagnant methods had a deadening influence on the students. He called them schools for death or dark schools, literally "the black school." Allowance must be made for his own adolescent apathy, but the rigid scholasticism was greatly in need of a challenge.

In 1829-31 Grundtvig made three trips to England, where he was greatly impressed by the English universities of London and Cambridge. He was fascinated by the openness and personal character of tutorial relations, which contrasted sharply with the rigidity of his own experience. At the same time he became intrigued with the busy folk-life of the English people, stirring and hustling in the early stages of the industrial revolution and immersed in a growing world trade. When he came back to Copenhagen these impressions compelled him to a thorough consideration of the relation of culture and Christianity, and he examined his budding thoughts on humanity in the introduction to *Nordic Mythology,* published in 1832. In this study he emphasized the significance of the mythological lore of Greece and the North in contrast to the legalistic rationality of the Roman approach to life, and he stressed the significance of oral communication, or "the living word." His analysis of a Christian

147

world-view, or *"Anskuelse,"* is commented on in our translation of a major portion of this introduction.[21] Important is the fact that he called for a "civic and noble academy," which should be "a higher institute for the culture of the people and for practical competence in all major subjects."

Plunging into the public life of his country, at first through writing and speech-making and later on through political activity and as a member of parliament, he developed his ideas and launched practical efforts toward the establishment of education for the people. In a variety of essays in the 1830s and 1840s he called for a higher school for people. By "higher" he meant adult in contrast to children, but he also meant that the school should inculcate appreciation of the higher arts, especially the language, lore, and history of the people. By a school of the people, or "folk high school" as he called it, he meant that the whole body of the citizenry was in need of enlightenment and inspiration, not just the elite or the selected few employed in civil service. The historic culture of the people would offer the greatest resources for cultural growth. Grundtvig called for a school that would not be shackled by entrance examinations and which should be open and available for anyone who had the desire and competence for participation. The educational method of the school should be the free and personal communication which had impressed him so in England. Traditionally this has been called "education for life" or "the living word," but, as K. E. Bugge has stated it in his definitive dissertation on Grundtvig's education ideas,[22] a better term would be "the living interaction," which, Bugge says, "is characterized by freedom, life, and naturalness."

We are not translating Grundtvig's first major educational essay, "The Danish Four-Leaf Clover," written in 1836 when the Provincial Estates began to function, for it is intimately addressed to the Danish situation. The four leaves of clover are king, people, country, and language. We begin rather with "The School for Life," written in 1838 when Grundtvig, who had been released from the restrictions of censorship placed upon him for candid expressions in earlier writings, felt free to influence public opinion. He tried also

21. See p. 26.
22. K. E. Bugge, *Skolen for Livet* (Copenhagen, 1965).

to influence the king, Christian VIII, who had a benevolent attitude toward Grundtvig's ideas, and he succeeded in persuading the king to establish a folk high school at Sorø.[23]   The next two documents included here are related to this ill-fated plan, for the polemics provided a vehicle for a further development of Grundtvig's ideas.

These ideas must be viewed in relation to the ongoing situation in Denmark, and their universal application must be deduced or distilled from this involvement.   They must be related also to his discussion of the innate validity of human living, and they must be seen in relation to his view of the Christian life as this is expressed in his writings on folk-life and Christianity.   In other words, the essays on education should not be read in isolation from his other essays.   An adequate study should also include consideration of four poems, or songs, which are related to education and which are included at the end of the section on hymns and songs.[24]

As the plans for the public establishment of a "folk high school" foundered, the ideas were picked up and put into practice by private initiative.   In 1844 a folk school was established at Rødding in the northern area of Slesvig, and it became a significant factor in the struggle against the encroachment of the German language and culture.   After the tragic war in 1864, when Prussia seized Slesvig, the Rødding school was reestablished at Askov, north of the new border, and it has been a prominent folk school ever since.   In 1850 the educational pioneer and innovator Christen Kold, who had emerged from the rural culture of Jutland but was inspired by Grundtvig's ideals, started a private folk school at Ryslinge, subsequently at Dalum, which became the prototype of a long series of folk schools established by disciples of Grundtvig during the next decades.   Grundtvig never became directly involved as an educator in a folk school except as a guest lecturer.   He saw them flourish, however, and this gave him great joy.   When an effort was made to establish a school bearing his name, he wrote a letter in reply to a friend who questioned the purpose of the school.   In this letter, which is included in this volume, he reiterates his ideas on education as late as 1854.

23. See "The Royal Decree," pp. 158–59.
24. See above, pp. 140–44.

The emphasis on a school for the people did not mean that Grundtvig was opposed to the university, although some of his repeated criticisms of its current function seem to imply this. He even proposed the establishment of a Nordic university at Gothenburg, Sweden. In an essay entitled "Concerning the Scientific Union of the North," written 1839, he developed this idea, excerpts of which are also given here under the title "A Nordic University."

The School for Life

1838

Translated by ERNEST D. NIELSEN

We all know, only too well, the kind of educational institution which I call "the school for death." Knowledge of schools of this type, which base their high repute on their great emphasis upon the "dead languages," is not limited to those who attended them. In this type of school they contend that grammatical perfection and the mastery of the Latin vocabulary constitute the very ideal of education. However, this idea can approach realization only at the cost and sacrifice of life. Indeed, "the school for death" is well known to all of our people. Without a single exception, every such school starts out with the alphabet and ends with book-knowledge, much or little as the case may be. Obviously, this includes every institution that we, throughout many centuries, have called a school, and still so designate.

Intrinsically, all "letters" are dead, whether written by the hand of an angel and with a heavenly pen, for every kind of book-knowledge which does not coalesce with a corresponding life on the part of the reader is simply dead. Until brain and body develop, subjects like mathematics and grammar, and all concentrated intellectual activity, have a stupefying and deadly boring effect upon children, for at that stage of human development they have neither sufficient knowledge of physical or mental life to discover it when mirrored in descriptive form, nor any natural inclination to be enlightened about its condition. Consequently, when we try to implant in children the sense of order and quietness, caution and wisdom, of those advanced in years, we inoculate them, figuratively speaking, with the infirmities of the aging person's decline in soul and body, resulting ultimately in death. In many instances, we completely destroy the adolescent's vigor of body and mind with the result that he finds ways of withdrawal. We thwart the development of human nature by defying its laws. . . .

This is in no way a farfetched notion of mine nor is it a mere lamentable opinion by experienced and humane physicians, especially in England and America. On the contrary, it is a thoroughgoing truth revealed to and confirmed by those whose eyes are keenly alert to man's everyday experiences and the course of contemporary history. The fundamental error which underlies the existing mania for pseudo-scholarship in our schools is, as some English physicians very correctly observe, the antithesis that we imagine to exist between the soul and the body. The consequence of this conjectured opposition is that whatever we strip from the body accrues to the soul. While neither the antithesis nor its consequences are in the spirit of Christianity, it cannot be denied that Christian writings and their shadowy image have imparted religious sanction to both. When the school, figuratively speaking, entombed us or misled us about our genuine human nature and smothered our vigor of life, our forefathers apparently comforted themselves by the thought that only the body with its totally depraved nature was subject to mistreatment and death. If only we had mastered the Catechism and the assigned Scripture passages as well as the best among our classmates, we were assured indeed of eternal life. Death was not intended as a separation from eternal life, but, on the contrary, offered the only way and desirable transition thereto.

Such superstition, even though disguised in a Christian form, is not apt to perturb or comfort many people in our day. What our forefathers attributed to that Christianity which can be learned from books and forced upon children, our generation usually ascribes to every kind of book-learning and self-reflection. They contend that this is an eternal gain for the soul, regardless of how ineffective and harmful it may prove to be in temporal life for body as well as soul, and, no matter how harmful it is for the development of competence, fully commensurate with our natural ability and aptitudes, and for the diligent industriousness upon which our temporal welfare, happiness, and sound reason depend, all of which has been provided by Providence and our biological nature. . . .

The Danish people's growing awareness of the urgent need for "a school for life" came to full expression at the Provincial Estates[25] recently held at Roskilde and Viborg. Both meetings showed that the feeling of need for educational change is quite general throughout Denmark. When the demand, nevertheless, is for more "schools for death," it is clearly a mistake which is easily explained. The error results partly from the want of a clear understanding of that particular life which the type of school that we lack presupposes. Moreover, it may be charged to the fact that the Latin schools, far from being willing to acknowledge their deadening influence on the students, on the contrary, daringly pretend to be the narrow gate that leads to life [Matt. 7:13-14]. In the usual Danish trustfulness this view has been and still is regarded as an article of faith. . . .

First of all, I shall now attempt to state as clearly as possible what I understand by a "school for life," because I have noticed that most people have not only very hazy but even erroneous notions about such a school. At the present a "school for life" exists, unfortunately, only as an idea and a projection. People think that such a school must be a center where the rules for the governing, the improving, and the effecting of the act of recreating life are persistently taught and emphasized—beginning, of course, by dissolving life, i.e., by death. It is a high German notion that life is explainable even before it is experienced, and that it must submit itself to change according to the dictum of the learned. Wherever this fanciful idea is incorporated into the educational structure, all such schools become workshops for dissolution and death where the worms live high at the expense of life itself. I completely reject this fanciful notion and maintain that if the school, as an educational institution, is to realize its potentialities for benefiting life, then this school, first of all, should not give the highest priority to purely intellectual activity or to its own institutional status, but set as its chief educational goal the task of helping to solve life's problems. Secondly, the school should take a realistic approach to life; it should strive to teach about life and promote purposeful living. Since there is no school that is able to create new life in us, the school should

25. Established in 1836.

neither tear down the old nor waste time devising rules that supposedly would be followed if only we possessed another and better life.

Man's activities display an immense diversity; yet, it is possible to view this bustling human life under three fundamental aspects: the religious or divine, the civil, and the scientific. Corresponding to each of these, one could conceive of three different kinds of schools for life: the church school, the public school, and the university, singly and collectively reflecting the distinguishing features of societal life. Just as the Estates, held in Roskilde and Viborg, stressed the lack of public education, so I, too, want to dwell on this subject because it deals with the one and only school which is open virtually to all of our people. All of us are obliged to become educated and useful Danish citizens, whereas the demand for professors and scientists is so limited, at any one time, as to provide few opportunities for appointment. If we only do not delude ourselves into thinking that religious or theological education can create a godly and Christian life where such is nonexistent, then it must necessarily follow that we have an abundance of both church schools and congregations, for where life is wanting, its enlightenment is really superfluous. In all probability, we have too many rather than too few, and too large rather than too small, institutions for the education of pastors and professors. However, we do not have a single institution for the adult Danish citizen! Therefore, even if all the schools within our system of education were excellent schools which fulfilled their designed purpose, the system would still be woefully incomplete as long as we do not have a school of adult education, a school, open to all, which will serve as a natural center for the fostering of all of our vital efforts. Any education which demeans and disregards this life is self-defeating, suffocates the people, and harms the nation. . . .

I readily admit that scholars regard this as gross heresy on my part. The Latinists insist, of course, that to excel in Latin one must treat Danish and all of its unique expressions slightingly. This must become habitual if one is to be well versed in the ancient language and to remove oneself from Danish barbarism to the classical world. The mathematicians, on the other hand, advocate a pure science which in reality cares neither for life nor for death, nor for any kind of human activity; even in its application mathematics is so universal and cosmopolitan that it can neither restrict itself to be a matter of language nor give special regard to the need and welfare of any single people or nation, unless the condition is present which gives the fullest possibility for the advancement and free exercise of pure and applied mathematics.   Without retracting my heretical view on science, which lies approximately midway between the positions of the man of letters and the man of science, I hold that the universal, human life in all its greatness—perpetuated from generation to generation—does not leave out but includes both peoples and the individual in every genuine and living scientific inquiry and task.   However, I shall deliberately avoid any scientific dispute and merely note that from my standpoint, as a person of common rank, our country and people are very poorly served by erudite men who shun their mother tongue, and the situation is not much better in the case of those for whom everything must be expressed in measurements and numbers. . . .

Therefore, even if there were no need in the land for a royal Danish folk high school for the general population, the need would still exist, especially for those whose education right from the elementary level has been planned to meet the course requirements of the Latin school.   For if the performance of those students in their future work as public servants or professional men is to be truly beneficial, they must be able to think and speak in Danish and to love and know their country and its fundamental laws as well as the best among their peers.   However, this will not happen unless they, through the folk high school, are given the opportunity to enter into living contact and personal interaction with a number of students of approximately the same age.   True, these students know no language other than Danish, but through experience they have acquired a far different kind of knowledge than that which can be found in any textbook, certainly not in those prescribed for use in the Latin school.   I am speaking of their personal familiarity with greater or smaller parts of the country, the people and the daily life of its citizens. . . .

If we agree that a Danish folk high school—royal, free, and

indigenous—is needed for the education of those who plan to enter some field of public service, what then about the education of that large proportion of the people that may not desire or qualify for such positions, yet must support both themselves and the public officials? The idea that those who constitute the nucleus of the people— agricultural workers, large and small independent farmers, skilled manual workers of every trade, sailors, and businessmen—do not need any training other than that which is gained behind the plow, in the shop, climbing the mast of a vessel, or in a place of business may be all right for barbarians and tyrants. However, this idea never has been acceptable to either the king or the people because it runs contrary to their Nordic way of thinking. Here, if anywhere, we are all of "one blood." Consequently, the same potential for educational and cultural achievement is discoverable in both cottage and manor house. This similarity of natural aptitude is particularly observable among the people of the Nordic countries where no foreign invaders took possession of the land and enslaved the old inhabitants. We cannot appreciate this too much. The common characteristics of the people are admirably suited to give them a much deeper love of country and a far more genuine culture than otherwise would have been possible. Despite the sad chapters in the history of our schools, it cannot be denied that a promising light broke forth with the Reformation and especially in 1660. Since that time, the school has been a liberating influence ennobling the boy from the very poorest home by opening the door for full educational opportunity and career advancement commensurate with ability of the highest order. . . .

Perhaps I might as well discontinue writing now as later, because for thirty years I have striven, impelled by Nordic vigorousness, to liberate myself from this whole foreign and spurious way of thought. In my own mind, it is all crystal clear. Yet, I doubt that I by my pen shall be able clearly to convey my thoughts to the reading public whose mind is deeply steeped in Roman thought. Readers seldom surmise what is involved. They usually fail to sense that there is no coherence between the Roman and Nordic thought, unless one regards the educated, elite world as a group of Romans who are intent upon having the rest of the world serve as slaves who themselves must earn their bread by the sweat of their brow [Gen. 3:19]. We can afford the support of public officials and scholars only if the life and work of these individuals contribute to the common welfare of all. In a period of rational thought the people will be of no mind to consent to such an outlay until we, by means of an indigenous, general education, on a continuing basis, enable them better to understand and appreciate the structure of our society and also help them to weigh the advantages and disadvantages of the various vocations as contrasted one with another. All the while, they will gain an education which will ennoble and elevate even the lowliest! People hue and cry themselves hoarse these days demanding liberty and education; it is unquestionably true that this is what we all need. However, the proposals that are made generally suffer from the same fundamental error that we find in Plato's *Republic,* in which the very guardians of freedom and education seize both. Thus, the people, in spite of all their labor, receive only the semblance of virtue and beauty for their enjoyment. The stark reality of this situation makes it incumbent upon the people that the citizens obey and supply what is necessary for maintaining the proud tyrants and, perhaps, find solace in the act of admiring and apotheosizing them!

The Royal Decree—An Explanation

by Johannes Knudsen

Before the Constitution of 1849 changed the government of Denmark to a constitutional monarchy with a parliament *(Rigsdag),* the nation was ruled by an absolute monarchy modified only by the establishment of advisory councils, or Provincial Estates, in 1836. It was under the absolute monarchy that Grundtvig's ideas about an institute for the education of the people, a so-called folk high school, had found favor with King Christian VIII (1838-48) and on March 27, 1847, the king issued a decree, which, among other items, established the desired school at the academy at Sorø, an idyllic town fifty miles west of Copenhagen. The academy had been a boy's school for two hundred years. Part 2 of the decree reads as follows:

> [The king decrees] that a higher educational institute for the real sciences be established at Sorø under the name "Sorø Real-Højskole," which shall have the purpose of working for the furtherance of these sciences in general as well as specifically.
>
> a. The general purpose of the "Realhøjskole" shall be to provide a higher and more complete education in the real sciences for those who have acquired a preliminary education commensurate with the courses in the real sciences. In particular it shall provide an opportunity to acquire a thorough knowledge of the language of our country, of history, statistics, and the constitution; in addition, for citizens in private occupations, of the most important parts of legislation and knowledge of administrative and community conditions.

Grundtvig was thrilled by this and wrote the essay "The Danish High School," which we reproduce in part. Before the school could become a reality, however, the king died, and the new king, Frederik VII, suspended the arrangement upon the recommendation of

his minister of culture, D. G. Monrad. In November 1848
Grundtvig was elected a member of the constitutional assembly, and
in this body he expressed his disappointment. The date was De-
cember 12, 1848, and the speech was directed as an inquiry to a new
minister of culture, the Latin professor, J. N. Madvig. This speech
is also included in our volume.

The Danish High School[26]

1847

Translated by JOHANNES KNUDSEN

I presume that I need not ask the reader to forget what I have previously written about this subject. I am sure he has never read it, and if he has, he has forgotten it without my encouragement. What I have written has never become a reality, for the world was against it. Nevertheless, I will request that the readers who remember what I wrote in "The Four-Leaf Clover" or "The School for Life" or "Prayer and Concept of a Danish High School" do what I have done: forget about it for the time being! The task is no longer that of convincing the government or my fellow citizens that we should undertake this effort; nor is it the task of disarming opponents. The task is not to show *how* the Danish high school, whose establishment His Majesty paternally has determined and royally commanded, can become a really new institution, unequaled in its quality, for the good of the people and the country, i.e., for the common good of all true Danes, from castle to cottage. Although we so-called scientists, full- or part-time schoolteachers, bookwriters, journalists, and above all tutorial drillmasters, critics, and reviewers, characteristically could not associate anything other than books and literary activity of our own making with the idea of a high school, His Danish Majesty, who creates a folk high school open to all, must necessarily think of the advantages to all of the people and all of the country. We do not need more academicians in Denmark, nor should a rational government wish for more book reviewers or stewards than crop up by themselves. Last of all could His Majesty desire to govern an entire people of so-called scientists, stewards, and reviewers. Although the image of a "learned republic," as

26. A section of the essay "Congratulations to Denmark on the Danish Blockhead and the Danish High School."

160

concocted by Holberg[27] or as current stardust, might seem even more attractive than a kingdom of the people, such a learned republic could never be a peaceful, lasting, flowering, and happy *Danish* kingdom, and the latter must, as a matter of course, be the goal of His Danish Majesty. By the establishment of a Danish high school such a kingdom will be brought about, certified, and undergirded. However, if the people and the country did not have the disposition and the resources for this kingdom, no high school or any other institution could create it, regardless of its wise character. The enlightenment of a people and the formation of its culture is a great work of art of whose magnitude the majority has no real concept. With the exception of the art of warfare, which is in itself destructive, every art, to be successful, must build on nature and must expect more from this source than from itself. Therefore, only because I know that the Danish nature is profound, rich, and fruitful in the sense desired by the king and all enlightened friends of the kingdom, I congratulate the king and Denmark on the occasion of the establishment of the Danish high school. I have only one prefacing remark, namely, that it becomes a really Danish school. It must never suppress, alter, or reconstitute the nature of the Danish people, but it must, by all efforts and by all means, to the best of its ability, be of assistance to this nature, so that this may gain strength, courage, and light and so that it may use the opportunity for movement, development, unfolding, and clarification.

The Danish high school must necessarily teach "the language, history, statistics, political science, legislation, and administration of the fatherland," but this is not enough. All this could easily take place in a stiffly formal, deadly, and boring, or even so un-Danish a manner that the school became an empty shadow or a national plague. Of shadows and plagues we have an abundance without the establishment of high schools.

At every high school of the people, which lives up to its name or which would be worth establishing even in the middle of Germany, the people and the home country must not be approached from the point of view of learning or of academic chairs, but rather from the

27. Ludvig Holberg, 1684-1754, gave a satirical description of the "learned republic" in *Niels Klim*.

requirements of life itself, and this means the life of the people. There must be concern for the very core of this life, its natural conditions, its diverse vocations, requirements, and industries. There must be an effort to seek whatever knowledge of country and circumstances would be possible and desirable, useful and enjoyable for all those who love their country and who have an average intelligence. Only then can we be sure that we are addressing all the people when we speak to them in their own tongue. Whether or not the impression they gain would be ephemeral or lasting, the effort would always be made with the right approach and for the good of people and country. . . .

What we therefore must seek to accomplish at every high school of the people is that all young men who attend and who already have found a vocation of their choice and competence could return to their task with increased desire, with clearer views of human and civic conditions particularly in their own country, and with an increased joy in the community of the people. This would encourage participation in all great and good things that have been achieved by their people and would continually be achieved.

In a human community there is always the obvious danger of inner dissolution, increasing conflict, and growing dissatisfaction with one's lot in life. Thus it is today, and the high schools of the people will therefore be both a necessity and a great help, inasmuch as their aim is to enliven and strengthen that love for country and that sense of community which ennobles and elevates as well as pacifies. The need is no less great in Denmark, where the ancient community of the people and the great love of country are the only profound sources of folk-life. Although we have done much in our blindness to block them, it is to be hoped that these sources will be inexhaustible. As soon as our eyes are opened we must hasten to reopen the fountains and, as far as possible, direct our efforts toward the ultimate limits in time and space of our domain. We must furthermore remember that even the minimum of that scientific attitude which would be essential in Germany would frighten Danish people away from the high schools. If we continue that game of playing schoolmaster, which is our constant temptation, we will irreparably harm the Danish high schools.

All this will become more evident when we consider seriatim the items mentioned in the royal decree about the Danish high school and the shape it must have in order to be suitable for Danish folk-life and useful for all situations. Too often our schools emphasize the benefits to individuals, even when these might be harmful to many, and thus we do more harm than good.

The *language of the country* is the first item mentioned by the king. This is right, because the mother tongue has decisive significance in all human education, even the most advanced, and because it has been downgraded as nowhere else in the cultured world. Although neither Germany, England, France, or Italy have duly appreciated their mother tongue for its value to humanity, the natural self-centeredness of these peoples, their great numbers, and other circumstances have prevented the neglect, abuse, and discard of their own language which is our situation. . . .

I know well enough that such talk about the mother tongue gives offense to many intellectuals, but this merely demonstrates that they are bunglers in their own language, despite their claim that they are great lights. In other countries intellectuals are well aware that they fall short when they do not master their own language. They know well enough that the mother tongue is a living expression of the unique character of a people, so that all the originality of even a genius has its root here. The cost involved is the very life of the people, when the mother tongue is scorned, suppressed, and downgraded so that it is used only in practical, everyday matters, used only in academies to introduce foreign and dead languages, as is the case with us, and constantly ridiculed because it expresses foreign niceties in a crude manner. The consequence will soon be that few people, or none at all, will be able to use the mother tongue in speaking or writing and that it will become a faint shadow of a foreign language. Then it will be dead and buried and it will float around like a spook. If our Danish mother tongue is not miraculously revived, it will soon be extinct.

Inasmuch as the mother tongue is the soul of the people, and inasmuch as its speech unites us with the people or separates us from it, the use and treatment of and information about the mother tongue is a major concern of the Danish high school. . . .

Books and book-learning will have to play a greater role, especially at the start, than they deserve. . . . This is readily admitted by one who, contrary to all his vexation at printed matters, nevertheless has his nose in a book early and late. . . .

Quite naturally our *ballads,* our *proverbs,* and *maxims,* with all their Danish imagery, their wisdom and innocent jest, must first of all be revived, dusted off, launched, and promoted, if we yet master them, or if we can discover their valuable property in hidden corners. . . .

Good Danish *books,* contemporary or future, which can be recommended to young people, will undoubtedly be promoted at the high school without my recommendation. I will therefore merely state that we need not fear that the Danish people will not ask for pens that "further their cause" when they learn to use their ears and their tongues. I must warn, however, that damage can be done when people are frightened by an abundance of books or when they are goaded to read them. . . .

The *history of the fatherland* is mentioned in the royal decree immediately after the language, and this is right. At the Danish high school the history of Denmark quite naturally will suit the mother tongue, but it will not be easy to get started. . . .

The matter in a nutshell is this: for the people the chronicle of the fatherland is neither more nor less than the "recollection of the fathers." This is the living narrative from mouth to mouth, from generation to generation, about the remarkable things that have happened in the country and to the country. The depth of love which a people has for its country can be measured by the living flow of this narrative with its high and low tides. . . .

I believe that the *statistics of our country* should be called "Denmark's mirror" at the Danish high school, or at least something similar. We should never burden people with foreign words, for they meet these too often. Statistics has no real place in the high school program, even when it is used rightly. It gives a static rather than a dynamic picture of the condition of the country. . . .

The *constitution of the country* has been a bone of contention for some time.[28] and it is quite remarkable that the royal decree included it as an item of study in the Danish high school. All friends

28. Denmark was yet a year or two away from its first democratic constitution.

of king and people must rejoice, however, for the Danish constitution is not a child of darkness but of light. The constitution can stand the light and like all living things it needs the light for a strong and fruitful development. . . .

The *legislation of the country*, as far as it concerns the common affairs of its citizens, is also mentioned in the royal decree as a course of instruction at the Danish high school. This is right, for it is important that every citizen in his total activity has knowledge of that part of the law that pertains to all. It is therefore doubly necessary that all those who are called for counsel on legislation have a clear view of the country's legislation and justice in order to express the will of the people in current legislation or in the revision of laws. . . .

Finally, *administration and municipal affairs* are mentioned in the royal decree as a course of instruction at the Danish high school. Such foreign terms are not in favor and they really belong under the study of statistics, or "Denmark's mirror," but they are still a matter of concern and need daily elucidation. The newly established national councils, county councils, and parish councils now parallel the function of state departments, county prefects, and sheriffs, and the opportunity for conflicts and confusion has grown. . . .

The danger of all precipitous and sweeping change is the inevitable clash of old and new, but the danger is even greater that the needs of a new order[29] are not discovered and supplied in time to prevent the disorder that will occur in traditional arrangements. . . . The first and great step will have been taken, however, by the establishment of a true Danish high school, and the second step will come when the Danish high school is combined with a nursery[30] for civil servants. These officials have many areas of activity in common with the people, and their education should be related to the people. No one should have spiritual or physical power without genuine appropriation. The Latin school and the university are the most unfortunate training grounds for civil servants. Such an expansion can readily be made, would inconvenience no one, and would do much good for all.

29. Representative democracy.
30. Training institute.

The Speech before the Constitutional Assembly 1848

Translated by ERNEST D. NIELSEN

It is in my mind's eye an extraordinary right that His Majesty has accorded all Danish *Rigsdagsmaend,*[31] when he empowered these men, who are accountable to the king and the people, orally and publicly to direct questions to his counselors. Precisely for this reason it is my earnest desire that both the Ministry and the entire, distinguished Assembly may understand that when I today, for the first time, exercise this right it is in no way personal, but a question affecting the people as a whole which I, as a *Rigsdagsmand,* address to the Ministry. This must of necessity be my most deep desire; yet, the destiny, accident, or whatever else we choose to call that inscrutable power, which especially this year[32] appears to have played its game with all peoples, has willed that the question which I today place before the Ministry of Denmark's educational system because of the high school in Sorø very easily may be construed as absolutely one of the most personal questions that possibly could be raised in the House. Therefore, I ask the honorable Minister and the entire distinguished Assembly to give me your kind attention as I strive to throw light on the subject of the importance to the people of the question which I intend to present today. Indeed, I dare presuppose this courteous attentiveness; for if I did not dare to make such an assumption I would be compelled to find myself completely useless here in the House. I am now an old, definitely independent person who does not belong to any of today's political parties. I am here in the *Rigsdag* solely for the purpose of speaking with old Danish simplicity and courage in behalf of the cause of freedom, the common life, and education; not, however, in that indefinite, gen-

---

31. Members of the Constitutional "Rigsdag" or Assembly.
32. 1848 was a year of revolution in Europe.

eral way which is currently popular and espoused by more than enough spokesmen, but to speak in behalf of this cause in its relation to time and place, its relation to Denmark and to the past and present condition of the people.

The high school in Sorø, which I am inquiring about, is, of course, the institution which King Christian VIII established during the last year of his reign [1847]; and he devoted his very last thoughts to this school which, however, seems to have been buried with him in his grave.   In accordance with his thoughts and decision, the high school was intended, on the one hand, to open the door for greater freedom in the study of the sciences than hitherto has been practiced here in Copenhagen; and, on the other hand, it should provide opportunity for all young people, regardless of class or occupation, to acquire a better foundation for the study of the mother tongue, and better instruction in subjects about their country and everything Danish than that which, up to the present, has been available through any publicly sponsored educational opportunity in this country.

It is this type of high school that I am inquiring about; thereby not implying, however, that I for my part believe that scholarship at our university or any of the other existing universities is practiced as independently and with that regard to the public good which the times require and I could wish.   However, that question is not at all before us; I am under no mandate to speak to it.   Even if my personal connection with the school in Sorø, or with the idea about the school, were to be brought up, which is unnecessary here, it never has been my thought or my proposal that the two should be mixed.

Succinctly stated, the object is an educational institution for all young people.   It was decided that such an educational institution should be established in Sorø where the existing physical facilities are fully adequate for its realization and present a befitting royal appearance.   Naturally, people will ask whether such an educational institution for all young people ought to be founded.   This school will aim at awakening their national consciousness, nourishing their love of country, instructing them in related areas at an early stage, and teaching them whenever feasible that we all, individually and collectively, and regardless of our social rank and occupation, belong to one people and as such have one mother, one destiny, and one purpose. It is obvious, therefore, that such a school, when it is nowhere to be found in a country, becomes the people's fervent desire, becomes something deeply wished for by those individuals who are becoming conscious of the indigenousness of the people; an awareness deeply felt precisely at a moment of time, which, like the present, constitutes a turning point—the greatest that can happen to a people.

It is a turning point which certainly is clear to all in this Assembly. We have been summoned here, as we know, to deliberate on a new constitution, that is, a new political foundation for the whole nation. Furthermore, we are called together also to deliberate on how to restore order once the old class distinctions have been abolished, and to envision how all may work together in a common spirit for the good of all. Yet, we must clearly recognize that among us, as with every other people in Christendom, it is not the majority only but even we ourselves who lack the clarity and the confidence which obviously are needed if this otherwise great task—the rebirth of a people—is to succeed.

Speaking in general terms, there surely is no question but that such an institution for the people's enlightenment, like that which was intended to be opened in Sorø, is well devised to meet the need of the times. Therefore, I am justly amazed, indeed, that the former responsible Minister of Denmark's school system at the very outset decided to let the idea lie dormant instead of effecting its realization. Unless all the rumors are false, it was his intention to close down the school completely. For this reason, I hope that the entire distinguished Assembly and the honorable Minister will recognize that even if I had not had the least part in developing the idea which should have been implemented, I still would have had the explicit obligation as well as the right to submit a question. The important question which I address to the present Minister, if it seem reasonable to him, is whether he plans to promote or hinder such an educational institution from being established.

Assuredly, I do not deny that in making this inquiry I am speaking with great warmth and seriousness of feeling and, I may add, with great anxiety for the awaited answer, because this institution has been my cherished idea thoughout a whole generation. It not only has been a subject close to my heart but one that I have reflected upon continuously. Surely, this is not, I think, unpatriotic. What other reason can I give for this heartfelt concern and reflection but that I am an old friend of the people and an old friend of the rural people. Consequently, I sincerely hope that Denmark's farmers not only may be praised for their self-restraint but may have the good fortune quietly to deliberate and discuss what, above all, concerns them; next, that they may reflect and express their views on general issues which may be for the common good of the entire people, while the rest of us are tempted to be attentive to that which is in the best interest—if not of any particular station in life or class, then, surely, in the interest of a particular vocation, a particular science, or field of knowledge.

I dare say this because the educational institution which King Christian VIII definitely spoke about and promised me the last time I saw his face, that institution, even if it were not to be organized in every respect as I hoped, was intended to be open to all regardless of station in life or occupation; its open door policy would have eliminated any painful entrance interview and required no entrance examination.

Regardless of my personal involvement in the destiny of this institution, I take the view that my involvement is a necessary obligation. Not only have I fathered the idea of the school throughout a long span of years, but I had hoped to devote my advanced years to the realization of the idea by contributing all my energy to that end. It was my hope that I also should see the high school founded by the king. He gave his royal word that regardless of what might happen, I should be given the opportunity at Sorø, in my advancing years, freely to prove whether the idea of the school was, as many believed, a brainstorm, a poet's dream, or whether it was in the people's best interest that such a school be established.

It is still worthwhile, I believe, to prove whether it is possible to create and nurture all indigenous, patriotic, and inspirational education open to all despite all the differences which, in so many ways, are observable both in our occupations and in our ways of thinking. Yet, there are boundary lines where we all meet, areas of common concern about which we all ought to be sufficiently enlightened and even as commensurately zealous in order to promote the common good for the benefit of the people and for the success of the nation.

A Letter Concerning the Folk High School to Peter Larsen Skraeppenborg in Dons

January 1854

Translated by JOHANNES KNUDSEN

I like this, said the preacher; they gave his children money. This is an old saying, as you, my old friend, must know. It is appropriate right now, for I like that you will not only give money but lots of it to the high school which my friends are helping me to establish. This is one of "my children," and when it is given birth it will be regarded by me in the most fatherly way.

What I like less, or rather not at all, is the fact that you have a dark and suspicious view of my intentions with the high school and the usefulness it might have. You may have valid reasons for this questioning, but neither old nor young authors appreciate it when their opinions are questioned after they have written books to make them plain.

What can we do about it? Is it reasonable to expect that a short letter can clarify what is still vague for one of my oldest, most diligent, and competent readers, despite my industry in books and journals? And you are in as basic agreement with me concerning human living and its rightful application as few others within or without Denmark.

I cannot be certain, of course, but a frank and "open letter," which is also a letter to a friend, gives more encouragement and opportunity for an author to express his opinion frankly and clearly than a general letter to everyone. In the latter case an author is not certain to whom he writes, about what his readers agree with him, or what language they are familiar with in a discussion of human matters. It is therefore worth a try to give you a satisfactory answer about the matter of a high school. I hope that this answer will proceed through your voice to the ears of many whom I cannot reach with my voice and for whom my pen is useless.

I will start with your assumption that the purpose of my high school was to teach young people to use their reason. You claim that this is important, inasmuch as it is undoubtedly terribly neglected in all other schools, where it is hampered more than promoted by rote learning and alphabetism.

The expression "to use one's reason" is not a favorite with me. I do not choose it or promote it in my writing about either church or school. In both of these situations it is commonly used to give voice to a view of human living and education which is far from mine.[33] I dare even say that this deviates from the truth or from the view of the Lord. I know, however, that when you use the expression and when it is commonly used by the people you mean to say that we must use common sense and consideration. This is exactly what I desire and hope that the young people will be encouraged to do at my high school and that they will be given better direction than they would at other high schools. This merely means that I intend to establish a real and decent school. It means that this school thereby becomes a Danish high school of the people. A school is not a real school if it does not promote common sense and consideration. It makes a great deal of difference, however, *for what* and *how* common sense and consideration are applied. Furthermore, "common sense and consideration" do not represent the *whole man,* and it is for the sake of the *whole man* that we need schools and churches. Whether I consider the educational program from the "purely human" side, which in my style is called the "Christian" side, or whether I consider it from the side of the Danish people, I conclude that we badly need a new school for our young men. I call this a "high school," not as a matter of pride or conceit but to indicate that this must be, in a decent manner, a free school for adults. It must strive to awaken, nourish, and clarify a higher concept of human living in general than is commonly held, and specifically of the life of the Danish people and the Danish citizen.

Dear friend, you are right that neither piety nor patriotism are school items. Such things are not spoon-fed. It is a poor school, however, that loses sight of these matters of the heart or puts them

---

33. Grundtvig is thinking about the age and philosophy of rationalism.

in a false light.   All good educators know this.   In their presentation of the general condition for human living and the sound use of human life they will make the students aware of the fact that when the human heart, which is the source of human living, is not there, all human education (enlightenment) is out of the question.

To awaken, nourish, and enlighten that human life, which is presupposed in Danish youth, this is the one and only objective of the Danish high school of the people.   If it uses the means that further this objective, it will be distinguishable from all other schools, high or low.   All of these have some form of book-learning as their objective, usually without any challenge to such learning's benefit or harm for the total human life of the student and certainly without consideration for the unique conditions, virtues and faults, advantages and disadvantages, of human living among the Danish youth, in contrast to the German or French youth or to a youth which exists nowhere on earth other than in the fantasy of sages who try in vain to make youth the same in all lands.

With this in mind I am sure you will agree with me in my conception of a Danish high school.   As a sensible man who looks realistically at life and seeks practical solutions, you will agree that our Danish youth not only need such a high school but will benefit greatly from it.   This is not only true when the young people wish to become Danish legislators or Danish officials; it is true when they are to become Danish human beings in all vocations.   For they are not to jump out of their skin but are to save it as far as possible and to live within it.   In order to do this they must be more familiar with themselves, their people, and their mother tongue than our youth has been awakened, helped, and shaped to be in any school up to now.

In regard to your final request concerning our inhuman and un-Danish schools for boys, I wish to do all in my power to change these schools as soon as possible.   Rather than preparing human enlightenment for adulthood, they hinder and prevent this.   If the schools for boys are to be changed, these schools will, above all, need good teachers who can and will put the change into effect.   Such teachers we can gain only by the education of young adults at a high school of the people.   A good school teacher with a human understanding is always a rarity. You seem to believe that by rules and regulations for teaching I will be able to inspire a number of school teachers who know that the schools for boys should be more alive and human than is now the case, but who do not know how to go about this. But an old "writer" such as I am has long since been cured of the superstition that the pen can change people or make them come alive, and I refuse to try this. What we can do, for the time being, for these schools is abolish the compulsion which daily erodes them and select the liveliest possible people as teachers. For neither of these actions do I have any competence, and neither will be effected until a higher human education has taken root in the young adults, making it impossible to continue the headless rote learning and the debilitating worship of the alphabet.

Finally, a few words about the "Danish Society" in the midst of our country, which you humorously compare to the "godly assemblies," called a church within the church by preachers.[34] I will stay within the metaphor and say that if the purpose of the "godly assemblies" was merely to acknowledge and to hold fast to that living Christianity which was maintained by only a few people despite the general membership of all, then they would correspond within the church to the function of the "Danish Society" within the people. It is the acknowledgment and maintenance of a living Danishness for which the latter is founded, a Danishness which is statistically allotted to all citizens but which is found in relatively few people. Both of these social relations[35] would then have their justification, and they can be a benefit to Christianity and Danishness. I do not consider either of these self-made relations so indispensable that I would "fight and suffer" to any degree for them. I am ready, however, to fight as hard and to suffer as long as possible for living Christianity and living Danishness. For me, as for most people in Denmark, the two are inseparable and for valid reasons. On the one hand, a living Danishness is always aware of the omnipotence of Christianity and its own impotence. On the other hand,

---

34. "Godly assemblies," revival meetings or spiritual group meetings, were often held where the local minister was strictly orthodox or a rationalist. The term "church within the church" comes from the expression *"ecclesiola in ecclesia"* used by the German pietist Philip Jacob Spener.

35. The religious and the national.

the spirit of Christianity always finds its expression in the language of the people in which he abides and whom he enlivens and enlightens. Christ himself made use of the human life of the people in which he lived and worked as a human being.

A Nordic University

1837

Translated by ERNEST D. NIELSEN

I must make every effort to delineate, as clearly as possible, the kind of union that I have in mind in order to be able to persuade both the elite and the common people of Scandinavia to desire and promote this union. Obviously, my proposal is for neither a church merger nor a political union of the people of each country, but a genuine scientific union. However, I beg the reader not to assume that he instantly knows everything that I have in mind on this subject. Hence, as a precautionary measure, I shall make the precursory comment that genuine scholarship, according to my way of thinking, is something far more than that which we associate with "black on white"; it is an educational enterprise of enlightenment which is not limited to the "printed page" but in a lively manner influences our thoughts and actions concerning all human conditions. In other words, all who are united in common scientific endeavors will strive through combined strength to defend life and liberty and employ them for the common good, and gain thereby that quiet clarity of thinking which is the crown of life. . . .

More specifically, what do I mean by a scientific union? I certainly am not advocating the introduction of a common, official written language; for as we take account of how even Iceland, a small and poor country, has adhered firmly to its own language, it becomes evident that we must relinquish any thought of either Denmark or Sweden discarding its particular written language. On the contrary, it seems far more reasonable to expect that Norway, in all seriousness, will attempt to develop its own, according to the unique characteristics of the spoken language. . . .

Because the Scandinavian, in the strongest sense, loves his mother tongue, it follows that he is capable and willing to love and appreciate every human language to the degree to which it is related to his own, and open to the understanding that the pen by no means is the master of the tongue; the pen is, in effect, only the servant of the tongue. To grasp this knowledge is the first step toward true scholarship. . . .

My proposal, yes, my sincere wish and fervent hope in this matter, is nothing less than the establishment of one large Nordic university to take the place of the four Latin universities with which we presently are afflicted. Of course, I can well understand that such a proposal must seem like a foolish daydream, especially to those readers who are unacquainted with or simply do not share my basic view on "the school" in general and on "Latin" in particular. . . .

If the reader will but grant me his brief attention, I shall attempt to show him that the proposal in no way is as fantastic as it, at first glance, is very apt to appear to many. . . .

My proposal for the establishment of one single Nordic university in place of the four Latin universities can demand consideration only in the event that the Scandinavian countries set up their own folk high schools and that the respective governments, on their own, discover to what degree the university education is irrelevant and inadequate for the preparation of administrative public officials— with the result that the governments would prefer their own training institutes and the folk high school. If such a scheme could be realized now, the well-being of the common and public sectors would be served aright. Moreover, the subject of the question under consideration would center around the one issue of how best to promote true and useful scholarship in Scandinavia; and then I would dare presume that people no longer would look upon my proposal for one, single Nordic university as a daydream, but find it worthy of thoughtful attention and consideration. . . . One Nordic university in place of the four Latin universities in Copenhagen, Upsala, Lund, and Christiania [i.e., Oslo]. . . .

At such a free Nordic university, whose seat the government should be obliged to declare a free city, the colleges or museums (in the sense of halls of study) should be divided into two types: schools of historical and of the physical sciences. Such a division would enable the colleges to pool their combined strength for an all-out scholarly effort and for the exchange of ideas.

Whenever I recall my experience thirty years ago at Valkendorf College [1808-11] or seven years ago at Trinity College [Cambridge University, 1831], I have a vivid picture of the incomparable fellowship that might be experienced daily at a free Nordic university where neither the old nor the young are restricted or conjoined in their movements.   On the contrary, everything which is spiritually exciting and awakening becomes the subject of lively discussions; and lectures and disputations, which as usually presented in the past did not coalesce, give way to well-organized scholarly and scientific conversations, partly with the young members and partly with those among the older members who willingly lend an ear to one another. If one first has such a picture of the everyday scholarly life and work at the Nordic university, it is easy to visualize how festive those gatherings will be if, for example, a scholar of first rank were suddenly to appear, and when other great events—such as the presence of distinguished visitors, of friends returning home from abroad, or of active and highly knowledgeable public officials in search of intellectual stimulation—were to set the spiritual "capital" [i.e., university] in full motion.

Now, regardless of how colorless this description may be, it probably will seem altogether poetical and fantastic to those who are unacquainted with any scholarly community other than our own university in its present form.   Only we who participated therein know that we, despite the most inauspicious circumstances, did catch a glimpse of this kind of scholarly atmosphere in this century. I witnessed the beginning when Henrik Steffens[36] stood among us [1802-3], and like a flash of lightning attracted our attention; and I saw the end when as a fellow at Valkendorf College in 1808-10, I associated with men like [Frederik C.] Sibbern and [Svend B.] Hersleb and was privileged to attend the social gatherings commonly held in the circles of the Ørsted brothers [Hans Christian and Anders Sandøe], old [Niels] Treschow and [Georg] Sverdrup.[37]

I can clearly see that it is to this glimpse of what higher education might be that I owe my own development as a scholar.   Later, yet in

---

36. A cousin of Grundtvig, Steffens brought the budding ideas of Romanticism to Denmark.

37. The men mentioned were renowned in the fields of culture, research, science, and public affairs in mid-nineteenth-century Denmark.

a similar way, it was my stay at Trinity College [1831] which by actual demonstration first taught me to understand how a collegiate fellowship can and will express itself when it is inspired by a genuine scientific spirit and keeps the mind's eye open for human life in its totality, its great natural laws, powers, and goals. If I were to experiment with this idea of a fellowship of scholars, I would merely survey, in retrospect, the lively quality of that scientific thought that ever flowered, namely, Athenian, in order to rediscover all those conditions that I would impose on a Nordic university. Under such conditions, I could not possibly overcommit myself or the Scandinavians, for the truth is that even as there were stouthearted and stalwart men among them in the past, so the spirit of the North is still a mighty force, and that the epoch of enlightenment for the whole human race, which the Greeks sought vainly to attain, now has caught up with us even before we became aware of it. . . .

While science, as pursued in university schools, strives in every way to include, enlighten, and explain the whole of human life in all of its parts and relationships, the cause of the indigenous common life of our people, on the other hand, which the folk high school serves, seeks in every way to strengthen, develop, and guide this life in effecting changes in sociopolitical directions so that its real needs and fair prospects may be met. Far from seeking to exclude collaboration, this separation, on the other hand, presupposes and requires a free exchange of intellectual thought, but it does ban the foolish practice of sacrificing life for the sake of book-learning, the mother tongue for dead languages, and the people for the schoolmasters. This separation, which I maintain is native to Scandinavia, is made here only. Moreover, this separation has been proclaimed and inculcated here from ancient times. When this separation, therefore, goes into effect among us, it inevitably must not only lead the way for great scientific advancements, but in a notable manner promote and vigorously safeguard Scandinavia's liberty, peace, and public well-being.

This separation, I maintain, can be actualized only when the Danes, Swedes, and Norwegians each establish their own folk high school, specifically designed to emphasize the mother tongue, national history, and the particular civil characteristics of the peoples, natural as well as historical. However, for the promotion of scholarship and science they should cooperate in the establishment and operation of a joint university because the spirit which permeates the North is *one*. A limited number of strong scholars, but sufficient for the task of a major university, should be selected; and the university, undergirded by adequate human and financial resources, should aim at making the Nordic philosophy of man effective in all areas. I finally affirm that by so doing the countries of Scandinavia will succeed in gaining whatever degree of unity they may desire. The unity must be strong enough to benefit civil liberty and autonomy and to combine the highest human spiritual qualities in all of their diversity of talents and knowledge for the purpose of effecting a powerful fermentation and lively cooperation in the whole realm of reality, especially with an eye to promoting a growing knowledge of Scandinavia and of all the conditions respecting the northern peoples. . . .

Times change and so must the patterns of man's work and life, but the spirit, which is undying, is ever the *same*.

BIBLIOGRAPHY AND INDEX

Bibliography

ENGLISH WORKS ON GRUNDTVIG:

Davis, Noelle. *Education for Life: A Danish Pioneer*. Liverpool: Williams & Norgate, 1931.

Knudsen, Johannes. *Danish Rebel*. Philadelphia: Muhlenberg Press, 1955.

Koch, Hal. *Grundtvig*. Translated by Llewellyn Jones. Yellow Springs, Ohio: Antioch College Press, 1952.

Lindhardt, P. G. *Grundtvig: An Introduction*. London: S.P.C.K., 1952.

Nielsen, E. D. *N. F. S. Grundtvig: An American Study*. Rock Island, Ill.: Augustana Book Concern, 1955.

Thaning, Kaj. *N. F. S. Grundtvig*. Copenhagen: Det Danske Selskab, 1972.

COLLECTIONS OF SOURCES IN DANISH:

N. F. S. Grundtvigs Udvalgte Skrifter 1-10. Edited by Holger Begtrup. Copenhagen: Gyldendal, 1904-9.

N. F. S. Grundtvigs Vaerker i Udvalg 1-10. Edited by Georg Christensen and Hal Koch. Copenhagen: Gyldendal, 1940-49.

Haandbog i Grundtvigs Skrifter, 1-3. Edited by Ernest J. Borup and Frederik Schrøder. Copenhagen: Hagerup, 1931.

Grundtvigs Skoleverden i Tekster og Udkast, 1-2. Published by Knud Eyvin Bugge. Copenhagen: G. E. C. Gad.

YEARBOOK OF STUDIES:

Grundtvig Studier. Published annually 1949-75 by Gyldendal (Grundtvig-Selskabet), Copenhagen.

Index

183